In the beginning......

We all come from indigenous peoples, it is only the time since we last realized that truth which separates us now.

My own family were primarily Celts from the dawn of time through the 1400's. We were born into and under a tribe, belonged to a clan, married into families and survived by basic hunting, wild-crafting and farming in the northern parts of what is now called Ireland. Our family was composed of Irish, Celts, Pict's, Scots, & Welsh of other tribes in a subsistence life.

Being on the 'border-lands' caused us to fight for our families and tribes, to resist many other tribes that came to conquer – the Vikings, the Romans and the English. Ultimately, we lost and survived only under the most severe of occupations in a starvation manner. Eventually, some of us left and ended up centuries later in rural northern Canada and what is now called the State of Maine in the U.S. Words and languages and customs had changed multiple times in that journey but we still held to our families, our ancestry and our stories to live once again in a new land of 'others' – and, still as farmers and hunters and gatherers.

400 years since that arrival, I have traveled the world and now settled in rural Alaska, once again with tribal peoples. What I find is what I have always known – ultimately, in our heart of hearts, we are all one people. In the intervening centuries from our 'beginning times' to now, each of the peoples and lands that we have been part of have brought different experiences, challenges, heartbreaks, joys and sometimes even different beliefs but not necessarily different character.

Despite whatever upbringing and teachers have told you, each and every group has a full range of human traits. All have members who are honorable and most have some that are despicable; All come from a family and most develop into a family; there is bravery and there are cowards; brilliant individuals and ones with difficulties; ones who seek wealth, others power and the majority seek respect. It has not been any different in the many countries and cultures I have seen through multiple decades.

I invite you now to take a short journey into the indigenous mind and heart. My sincerest hope is that this small book, in some way, brings in to focus where we all came from and helps us get to where we are going with as much peace and respect as can be mustered.

Christopher 'kaskae' Wright

Original copyright under the title <u>Pace and Presentation: Protocol with Tribes and Indigenous People; A Primer for Business</u>
© 2002 by Christopher 'kaskae' Wright, TXU 945-448 – title under amendment

Permission to copy or use any or all parts of this material for educational purposes may be granted with written or electronic permission of the author.

All pictures/drawings were personally created by the author or are public domain.

Front Cover:
    Fishwheel: A fishwheel is a salmon catching device available to every Alaskan although they can be used on only 6 rivers. Mostly they are homemade devices used for subsistence. This particular wheel was built by Johnny Goodlataw, myself, and many volunteers, at the 2009 Tazlina-Chickaloon Culture Camp. This wheel is presently viewable at the Wrangell-St. Elias National Park and Preserve HQ in Copper Center, Alaska.
    There are varying stories concerning its invention citing China and Scotland. In North America they were first seen in the rivers of the east coast in the 1820's and later in Northern California and the Pacific Northwest. Nowadays they are in legal use only in specific Alaskan rivers.
    The current pushes the paddles in a circular motion, the fish swimming upstream get caught in the baskets. As the basket rises, the fish slide down an incline plane to a basket on the side.
    On my very best single day during the salmon runs, I pulled in (and had to take care of) over 400 King and Sockeye salmon, averaging about 7 lbs apiece but with some Kings running in the 40-50 lb range.

Johnny's Tazlina Wheel

Chris (author) & Floyd's wheel

Preface
"Elip Chee Mamook"

Nomenclature: There are many terms and identifiers by which Native people are known. Each group has it's own specific name, that which it wishes to be called, as well as well as a regional or language based term, and then there is the name that other people give them. In addition, in certain cultures, people may belong to a clan system as well as a family grouping. For example, a person may simultaneously be a tribal member of Tazlina Village, be a member of the Caribou clan, be a shareholder of the Ahtna regional corporation, speak a derivative of the Athabascan language and be generally known as part of the Dene' culture.

For the purposes of this presentation, global and generic terms will be used interchangeably. First Nations, Indigenous, Aboriginal and Native will all represent the first known people of that particular land.

By the same point, non-natives also come in many stripes and divisions. For the purpose of this presentation, they will primarily be identified as holders of the western worldview or western way of thinking. For simplicity of expression, the western worldview will be that mode of thinking that is dominant in North America and Europe – one of Aristotelian logic, rationality, segmentation and linear patterns as typified in the pursuit of science.

Format: Each section is divided into four parts. Each part is meant to introduce the subject in a different yet compatible manner. The main section may focus on history, background or even neuroscience to make its point. The second section, titled "In Short" is a plain language synopsis of how the first section works in real life. Section three, "Applications" provides a few examples of how the first two sections might be applied. The final section, "See also" refers one to other areas of the manual which are related or similar.

Caveats: References for this presentation rely primarily on personal experience, conversations with Elders and research of academic resources related to the far northern hemispheres and the high & sub-arctic regions in North America, Scandinavia and the USSR. It is the author's experience that the basic applications apply throughout the planet. However, despite the television commercials, one size does not fit all. Each group, each individual is exactly that – a unique entity that is a composite of the totality of that person or groups experiences over time.

This manual is only intended to stimulate thinking in a manner that will facilitate interactions with Native people, be they business or personal and, as this book describes, these interactions are so intimately intertwined with cultural values in most Native cultures as to be almost one and the same thing. The book is meant, in short, to help prevent the reader from stepping on his/her own tender appendages and blocking further positive interaction. It is simply much easier to offend than to make up for offending.

The interested reader is encouraged to read the source material where indicated. Rupert Ross' classic book, "Dancing with a Ghost: Exploring Indian Reality" is out of print but can be found in some public and many university libraries. Hugh Brody's experiences are commonly available and his latest book, "The Other Side of Eden" is an exceptionally clear and easily read resource. I am personally indebted to each of these authors for their ability to translate northern experiences across the multiple barriers of culture to my own mind. It is their writings that have given me the energy to be one more cautious interpreter for speaking of these wonderful cultures that have so deeply enriched my experiences on this plane.

It has been said that there are simply too many individualities among Native peoples to write a single book based on commonalities. My experience does not agree with this. As beings on this planet, we hold many more commonalities than differences. The problem develops because we tend to place emphasis on the differences, not the samenesses. The western way of thinking is reductionist, it reduces and thereby separates rather than bring together.

The odd words under each chapter heading are Chinook Jargon or Chinook trade language. This language, as the name implies was a pidgeon language developed by early traders and trappers in the Pacific Northwest that was used for communication from Alaska & Canada to the Midwest and down to California. In the way that this was understood across nations, so too I hope this book will be— imperfect but functional.

Table of Contents

Prelude

The author has been perplexed throughout the writing and presentation of this book, by the resistance of wise and worldly experts to accept the concept of both commonality and uniqueness as a logical expression. I understand the literary confusion – it can be a cumbersome idea to get a handle on.

Uniqueness, by definition, is a singularity, one of a kind. Commonality is a collection of shared traits – or history – or biology – or even experiences. The expression of each of these words in the same sentence seems to compare to the rule of physics that two objects cannot exist in the same space at the same time.

Origins and Unique Commonality

Western science, by its nature and developed rules, is primarily reductionist – reducing things to individual components. It separates by differences in order to study and understand one thing from another thing.

There are many classes of living creatures on the earth which western science has divided into categories – mammals being but one. Mammals are not even the largest category, nor even the most numerous but it certainly interests most of us as that is the grouping in which humans reside and we are almost all curious about ourselves and each other. What are we made of, why do we do what we do are philosophical questions of the ages.

Western science has brought many useful and even wonderful understandings (and a few not so wonderful ones) that have had major and minor influences on our lives and histories.

Yet, reductionism is the study of differences and the emphasis on our differences meshes with much of our conscious and unconscious memories that have kept humans disunited as a species and inhibited both our growth and our survival as unique beings. It focuses on the rather minor differences at the expense of our very substantial commonalities, unhappily creating the environments for bigotry, war, oppression and fear.

Origins and Unique Commonality – 2

Humans, homo sapiens, are the mammals that have transversed millennia from rather rare, relatively weak creatures to a dominating and powerful population that controls (and may be extinguishing) the future survival of mammalia on this planet.

Let's look at humans as we might look at snowflakes or fingerprints. It is believed (I don't believe it has ever been 'proven') that each person on this planet has singular fingerprints. It may or may not have been validated in the 130 or so years that we have been actively looking at fingerprints but it has been verified sufficiently that guilt or innocence can be based on it throughout the judicial world.

So, the difference in one aspect of our skins can certainly establish some level of uniqueness for each of the billions of humans as individuals. That one aspect of humanity itself powerfully helps prove that we are each unique – but does it prove we are all different?

Western science, in the modern marvel of genetics, has shown that while individually unique, human DNA shows that we are composed of some 99.95% of the same base materials. Certainly this validates the most basic of commonalities.

Whether you follow recorded history, faith, religion, mythology, science or any other form of looking backward in time, all cultures (grouping of humans with a perceived or identified similarity) have a story of origin – a place where humans started. Whether your particular belief is that the first humans were a smarter chimpanzee or that we appeared whole from some source, created by a god or resulted from an accidental mating of two other species, or even were imported from another place in the universe, there is a common set of beliefs that humans had a beginning – another basic commonality.

Despite our advancement (?) as a species, individual humans remain a fairly fragile and weak entity compared to the forces of nature and environment we often face. Individual humans would inhabit a pretty short and harsh life should we be bereft of other humans in almost any part of the globe. Humans have always had to band together in order to accomplish anything beyond a most simple existence. In fact, should we not band together in the most basic act of mating, we could and would not have survived as a species at all.

Origins and Unique Commonality – 3

Whatever your belief system, civilization(s) did not start with cities, or even villages. They did not start with Kings or Emperors or Presidents. Working and living together probably started with families.

Kinship groups were undoubtedly the initial and primary form of group survival. Despite probable differences in size, shape, skills and physical abilities, there was at least a bond developed and enhanced by child rearing, history and interdependence – as well as being able to simply recognize each other. That may seem simplistic but the basic reality of knowing each other over time vastly increases the options for survival compared meeting with another human omnivore whose desires and wishes are not known to you and may not enhance your own survival.

Simple kinship groups, however, both enhance and deplete survival. Due to some of the known peculiarities of the genetic material that families share, survival of offspring is tied to mating outside of the basic family group. Groups, of necessity, cooperated to some degree with each other to vitalize offspring and enhance the size of the groups. As long as the food supply permitted, groups could grow and become more adept at both procuring and defending.

Basic grouping was strongly related to kinship ties and to propinquity (being near each other). Propinquity is important for a very similar reasoning that families are – knowing each other over time – being able to predict, and therefore realistically plan. Eons later, in our modern world, propinquity is considered the main force in the creation of groups – simply being around someone is necessary to develop the basic trusts to proceed further in relationships – whether it be neighborhood watches or marriages.

Initially, I am sure, we chose those who were like us somehow – the more similar the easier the integration. Similarities in language, history, habits, beliefs as well as physical traits probably counted highest. Choice was not always an option though – rape, war, kidnapping probably played a significant role as groups grew larger and territories intercepted each other. It was, as far as we know, always within the same species (another genetic requirement, it seems) but recent studies with Neanderthal DNA has even put that in question.

As groups grew, contact and interaction grew between ever increasing number and variation of groups with a multiplicity of degrees of similarities and differences. Vestiges of those initial groupings based on safety and need survive well into modern times based on such things as culture, religion, race, and history. Yet, the world population has simultaneously grown so geometrically that interaction and mutual knowledge have effectively dimmed, and sometimes erased, what were once perceived as vital differences.

Propinquity – that other basic form of necessary interaction has also changed. Rather that defined in miles, it is not even necessary to define it in continents but can exist as belief systems or internet connections. While we retain our personal histories and group identities, humans are ever less limited by the differences and required at most levels to recognize the commonalities.

The Range of differences within groups is larger than the range of differences between groups. First noted by Charles Darwin and validated by many other social and biological scientists, is that the range of differences within a group is often as large, or larger, than the range of differences between groups. There can be a wide *variety of anything within a certain group that is actually quite common with another group but the differences between the groups themselves is not necessarily much more than minor.*

Simply, while we retain identities based on differences, we rely on commonalities for the same safety and enhancement reasons that groups developed in the first place.

Origins and Unique Commonality – 4

Race is a social construct, not a reality. The more obvious or visual a difference is, the more it is identifiable as 'other', though the color of skin is, in reality, less a difference than such things a culture, belief systems, and personal history and environments.

One validation can be seen in the changes in the definitions of race in merely the previous century. In 1910, Jewish, Polish, Irish and Slavic peoples were all considered different races – in fact there were dozens then. Now, in 2007, we seem to be down to the 4 most visible, and also the most ludicrous: White, Black, Brown, Yellow. Geneticists have clearly noted almost no differences in the human genome that identifies races.

What people are really concerned with, rather than race, is culture. Culture is defined as a common history, customs, values. Culture is the definer of much of our grouping habits. What we don't understand, we isolate and segregate.

In and of itself, even this grand commonality is somewhat illusionary. This is because the basics of cultural differences are often only the expression of those parts which are deemed culturally distinct. What I find is the sticking point on cross-cultural relations mainly comes down to priorities – the importance to the individual or the group of whatever is being confronted or discussed or seen. However, those cultural expressions are deeply embedded.

So, please read on, and decide for yourself

Introduction

"Chee Klatawa"

"Most people would rather die than think; in fact, they do so." Bertrand Russell (1872-1970)

I didn't come to the North Country totally unprepared, or am I fooling myself? Life in the sub-arctic and high arctic is a life like no other and life in the _indigenous_ north is yet another step removed in both time and space.

In our lives, whoever we are and wherever we come from, we develop a belief in a reality that we deem immutable. This is how life is and we operate our existences based on what we think we know about the commonalties and limitations of the universe around us. As we get older and continue to survive, these beliefs become entrenched as Truth, and we seldom stray from what has worked for us. It seems that we have dipped into the universal mind and snagged a Reality and we hold onto this one piece of surety to guide us through our slice of living.

The Far North changes all of that. Without apology or forgiveness, the extensions of the far Northern Hemisphere thrusts one into an alien world – not only of landscape and weather but also of core concepts of time and space, of reality itself.

The impetus for writing this particular book came out of frustration, disappointment and sadness, not particularly or solely my own. Countless times I have watched representatives of various aspects of different cultures, people with good hearts, products and intentions, fall flat on their faces in the very first interchange. So often, the intent was well meant, with both sides initially desirous of linking with the other. What which each side had to offer would have been mutually advantageous and productive with both financial and cultural gain for all parties. The failure of these interactions was unnecessary and the barriers created would be long-lived.

The failures of mutual understanding were unnecessary because, at least at one level most of us know that cultures and cultural differences exist. The problems in these interactions seems to be that the longer we are successful in our own _culture_, and the less we stray out of it, the more tunnel-visioned we become in seeing the reality, the validity or the power of other cultures.

The immersion of culture probably begins at birth, perhaps even before. The power of culture is reinforced, reiterated, and restated with most every interaction in our young lives by the significant peoples physically & emotionally close to us. From our first exposure to daylight, we are constantly taught and reminded of the meanings of expressions and gestures, of positive and negative actions and their concomitant responses, of voice tonality, odors, tastes and environments – of color, symbols and interactions. We mimic these significant others to gain their approval and security and, after years, move outside of our nuclear environment to enter schools – again of mostly like-trained individuals, to gain further instruction of the definitions of 'we', 'us', and 'our'.

Then it happens. Somewhere along the way, we run into the 'other' – someone of a different background, values and beliefs. At the most benign, depending on our own cultural teachings, the 'other' promotes curiosity or intrigue. However, depending on the environment, the actions and the training of our culture, the response can just as easily be related to defense, threat or fear. Our defense mechanisms move into gear. In a dichotomous culture, that which we know as 'normal' must be right; therefore, the other must be wrong.

But, we are enlightened, are we not? We have been taught that we have been brought up in the most advanced, proper, historically validated society on earth and have at our disposal all the tools of that training and education. If we are strong and superior, then we should not fear the 'other' so we must create within ourselves, some form of validation of why the 'other' is the way he/she is – and the creative myth making begins.

This _dichotomy_, that things are simply one way or another, is the simplest, most primitive decision-making tool of _Western_ cosmology[1]. Based in the evolutionary history of survival, life and death decisions must be made in seconds – fight or flight; right or wrong, good or bad, black or white, yes or no – they are our first and very powerful defense.

As our life and intellect advance and experiences increase, gradations of these simple rules of decision making come into existence. Not every incident has life or death consequences and the grays between the extremes continue to widen. We seek reasons and explanations for the differences and, with proper guidance, perhaps knowledge and wisdom. However, without the proper guidance or natural bent, knowledge will not necessarily produce wisdom and we find ourselves once again sitting on Occam's razor.

William of Occam, English philosopher and excommunicated Franciscan monk is incorrectly credited with this several hundred year old logical theorem and base rule of scientific modeling which admonishes us that when choosing from a set of otherwise equivalent models, to choose the simplest one[2].

The simplest choice is most commonly the choice that fits comfortably with our existing knowledge and/or beliefs. If our existing knowledge is predominately one cultural folkway which we hold as sacred or, at least, right, then, by Occam, other cultures must be attributed with such things as inferiority, backwardness, primitiveness or lesser evolution. In the world of A.A., this is called 'stinkin thinkin'[3][4]. This is known as a logical fallacy in that it may be true in logical format but not correct in functional life. It could be just as true that the 'other' might be superior, advanced or more evolved but that would require a rethinking of our own culture and make things much more complicated.

This oversimplified set of logical assumptions fails to actually explain anything, to give a 'why' for the differences that a significant group of fellow humans follow. Merely through their continued existence, other cultures must have some strong and positive value to their adherents in order to withstand the onslaught of forceful dominating powers over hundreds of years.

To complicate matters even further, many non-Native Westerners may not even recognize that North American First Nations often have differing values and institutions that remain valid and relevant in their lives today. The concept of the American melting pot further reinforces this lack of knowledge in many non-natives. As the title of this work suggests, although Natives and non-Natives share common human needs and desires, how we set out to meet these needs and desires is often very different.

It is my hope that this book will do several things for the interested reader. It is not my intent to fully explain _Indigenous_ cultures, and I doubt that would ever be realistically possible. It is difficult at best, if not virtually impossible, to ever fully see through the eyes of a culture different than one's own. Rather, my hope is only to tweak some existing understandings sufficiently to allow for a modicum of conceptual change. Along the way, some understandings of the 'other' may appear, some myths may be seen in a different light, and some grievous errors may be avoided.

Even the choice of creating individual, segmented chapters for the Western reader has built-in flaws regarding coherence. One chapter may help with a single piece of focus, but only in relation with thoughts appearing elsewhere, will the necessary depth and breadth be, hopefully understood.

History is replete with poor relations between _Native_ and non-native people. We cannot change the past. In the interest of interconnectedness for both worlds, it no longer makes any sense for either culture to isolate from the other. We do not have to be alike, and need not be – optimum survival requires diversity. Each group can find benefit in the knowledge of the other and it matters little which format we take – only that it proves positive. We may not have a common heritage, but we do have common challenges in an ever-changing world and each may have the resources the other needs.

If the purpose of interaction is to have a positive result, then, in obverse, we don't need to be wasting our time in unsuccessful ventures. If the reader wishes to know more of the 'why' of these differences, references for this purpose have been provided at the "Table of References" for each chapter. Many authors have done much more thorough explanations in their works than I could provide. This publication is intended only to impress that differences do exist, and they exist for good and sufficient reason. Your choice is whether you can accept and work with those differences.

The generalizations that follow in each chapter are just exactly that – generalizations! Each community and individual is unique, as the reader will be reminded throughout this work. In any one village you will likely find individuals at many stages, skills and accomplishments in a range of endeavors and sophistication that are intra-cultural, cross-cultural and trans-cultural and have ideas and understandings that transverse traditional to Western processes.

RULE #1
"Mamook Kloshe Ikt"

The first and most mandatory rule that absolutely must be followed in all aspects of cross-cultural communications belies its' simplicity. Welcome to the minefield of intercultural exchange. This is not a minefield laid actively and directly by persons of ill intent but rather a semi-natural consequence of a lack of knowledge of sensitive areas, dangers and pitfalls within previously unknown territory.

There is no need to explain that there are cultural differences. The study of cultural differences is also not strictly the purview of ivory tower academics, social scientists or international governments. Anyone who meets and interacts with people outside of his or her normal social and business circle has to have a basic understanding that there may be difficulties and that success depends on treading softly.

The worlds of indigenous peoples are vast, complex, multi-faceted and coherent. There do exist various threads of commonality – both within and across cultures – as we are all descendents of the family of man. There do also exist vast chasms of difference in the expression and importance of untold aspects of life – of methods of examination, levels of valuation, styles of learning, consequences of actions and internal belief systems.

The unnumbered range of differences among Native people is as real as the threads of commonality are. One does not negate the other nor does one necessarily explain the other. In every situation, however, application is the key. Successful application is knowledge based on observation, experience and a deep and profound understanding of Rule #1.

This book, as with all other books you will ever read on cross-cultural interactions is incomplete. The problem is that the rules of social behavior are not very exact nor are they uniform across societies, tribes, cultures, groups or even individuals within a group. In fact, the same interaction in one group may have opposing reactions in another. The simple fact is that THE rules of social behavior don't exist. Rather, there are many rules of social behavior.

For one example, I will draw upon some personal experiences of the expressions of silence in interactions. Among the Northern Athabascan (Indian) groups I am familiar with, taking a relatively long period of quiet, internal reflection previous to speaking is seen as polite, respectful and indicative of taking the time necessary to organize your thoughts in a useful and clear manner. This particular protocol is the same for the speaker as it is for the audience.

In the same area of Alaska, lived an Apache man with his descendents. This man was born in the late 1800's into a traditional band on a new reservation in the American Southwest. As Apache's are also considered part of the Athabascan group, I would often talk with him about the customs and behaviors that I was learning about. On the subject of silence, he remembered things as very different within his band. He saw proper protocol as the need for the speaker to be quick witted and unhesitant in his speech though the audience could and should retain considerable quiet time for analysis and comparison of the speaker's words. For the speaker to be slow and quiet, he said, showed a lack of heart in the subject and possible manipulation in the way he would speak to one audience as compared to another. This was especially true, he stated, among warrior societies. He would always tell me that a warrior's way must be straight and true, direct and without fear, from his heart to his words, to his actions to his death.

These are both Athabascan examples yet they are not the same, and the story doesn't end here because so many of the things that I call Chapters seldom stand alone without relationship to other aspects of culture.

Expanding on the chapter on Languages and within the same context as the preceding paragraphs on Silence, the conundrums multiply. In the same Athabascan universe, there are differing ways of presenting depending upon the presenter, the formality of the circumstance and the situation. If one was to take a look at the book, "Tatl'ahwt'aenn Nenn': The Headwaters People's Country, Narratives of the Upper Ahtna Athapaskans" one finds many examples of 'high' or very formal language usually reserved for important and delicate subjects of ceremony and cultural history. Whereas 'high language' may be used in public speaking on certain subjects, it would not be normally used in a corporate presentation, nor at a village council meeting where other, less formal renditions apply. In daily life within a village, one may hear formal, conversational and pidgin versions of the local dialect of the regional language. In each of these uses of language, the definitions of the words are unchanged but form and style may change the emphasis or valuation of the subject at hand.

But we are not yet done with the various threads of communication that are woven into the seemingly simple, relatively short interchange. Elders have their own patterns of interaction, which can change dependent upon audience. Whereas, among equals, their interchanges can run the gauntlet from the easy informality of lifelong friendships to serious, contemplative direct communication to extreme formality. When they are imparting lessons to learners, the methodology is often indirect narrative where it is the listeners' responsibility to glean the important parts.

This is still not all. We started this conversation with a simple set of examples on the uses and recognitions for a simple silence in one relatively small grouping of Athabascan people. Still to come would and could be the effects this silence imparts with the use/lack of gestures and body movements, or the style of dress and place of presentation, or age and relative status.

Multiply this now complex web times the thousands of varying groups and sub-groups of aboriginal peoples throughout the world and you have begun to understand the essence of Rule #1.

Even within one's personal culture, one where a lifetime of learning and practice has occurred, a person would be hard-put to list all the nuances of proper behavior in all potential circumstances. Luckily, there are likewise avenues of apology and forgiveness, which we can employ to alleviate the situation. This too, is not guaranteed in another culture, and most likely not done in the same form.

At this point, if you are not thoroughly confused as to what you should do and when you should do it, you probably shouldn't be reading this book. If, however, you find this terribly complex and confusing, Congratulations! You are one of the few that understand Rule #1.

Rule #1: There simply are no hard and fast rules that govern all or even most situations between cultures.

While Rule #1 tells us that pitfalls and difficulties exist, it doesn't deny that there are maps of conduct and avenues of information that can assist the cultural explorer in positive and beneficial ways. Throughout this book, these cautions are repeated in multiple ways as are the concepts that we each want conscientiously applied to ourselves in our home worlds – concepts of respect, tolerance and gentle honesty. Accompanied by astute observation and cautious treading, these three will light the way to worlds of immense beauty and other visions of wisdom that will benefit us all.

CHIEF WILLIAM OF TANANA   PAUL WILLIAMS, TANANA   CHIEF CHARLIE OF MINTO
CHIEF ALEXANDER OF TOLOVANA   CHIEF THOMAS OF NENANA   CHIEF EVAN OF KOSCHAKAT   CHIEF ALEXANDER WILLIAM OF TANANA

Alaska State Library - Historical Collections

Tanana Chiefs at 1915 meeting

Alaskan Federation of Natives, 2007

Who and Why?

Kalk'-sta – Kah-ta
"If you chase two rabbits, both will escape." –Anonymous

All societies have a structure – both one that is visible and one that is functional underlying the visible. Due to the regulations of mainstream society, many positions, titles and organizational aspects have legal definitions, requirements, rules and functions. These legal definitions constrain the visible structure of organizations.

However, the less visible structure – often called names like corporate culture or the power behind the throne – may have the final say on who is authorized to do what, where and when despite formal job descriptions. In the ebb and flow of business and cultural change, these lines of influence also change.

Cultures are dynamic – they have to be in order to survive. Just because *aboriginal* history is ancient does not mean that indigenous cultures are static. As with all successful enterprises, aboriginal people will incorporate that which works for them, in a way that is harmonious with their way of thinking.

While most Native societies are *collectivistic*, there simultaneously exists an ultimate individual freedom within them. Each person has a view of the universe that was given specifically to him. The image most Westerners have of Native culture, especially combined with the rule of consensus, is an image of required uniformity. Actually, the Native world is the opposite of uniformity in the practice of individual freedom. The ability to see or know differently and to share that unique knowledge is appreciated and encouraged, but decisions affecting the group will usually not go forward without the combined wisdom of the group in agreement.

Who are you dealing with? There are many facets to the Native economic world - village corporations, non-profit corporations, regional for-profit corporations, subsidiaries, private businesses, partnerships, joint ventures and collaborations to name a few. Sophistication, education, need and desire are different in each group, and not always in any expected order.

In Alaska, for example, almost all Native villages are individual, federally recognized tribes. These tribal entities may or may not join legally in some or all aspects with a regional corporation for efficiency or power reasons. These organizations are usually intimately related, sharing board members and working together on independent or mutual projects. However, each may have their separate agenda. Each will make its own decision concerning its entity.

Regional Corporations: Profit: In Alaska, the Alaska Native Claims Settlement Act (ANSCA) of 1971 created an initial settlement of $962.5 million with 44 million acres of land and 12 regional Native corporations to represent Native populations of Alaska and one 'virtual' corporation to represent Natives not living in Alaska[3].

These twelve corporations usually contain the coalescence of the top levels of Aboriginal controlled technical and legal expertise in a region. They are 'for profit' entities, often with many subsidiaries and interconnections. They are responsible to their shareholders, give dividends and often represent or assist villages in land and other issues.

Regional Corporations: Non-Profit: Most regions have also developed a non-profit corporation which primarily serves Health and Social Service needs for member villages and individuals. Substantially funded by the Department of the Interior, Bureau of Indian Affairs, Public and Indian Health Services, these groups also secure secondary funding via public and private grants, loans and miscellaneous activities.

Housing Corporations: Funded primarily by the U.S. Department of Housing and Urban Development (HUD), these independent Native run organizations are known as Tribally Designated Housing Entities (TDHE's). TDHE's are the primary construction entity for residential housing in or for Native communities. If construction is your focus, a thorough reading of all 600 pages of NAHASDA (Native American Housing and Self Determination Act) and supplements is in order.

Village Corporations: Some villages did not join regional corporations and retained their own control of land. Some did join the regional corporation but limited their relationship to specific areas.

Village Councils: Villages are independent governing bodies within a region with varying formal connections to the other organizations. They are usually governed by an elected council which represents the particular village interests, fund activities and oversee organizations operating within the village boundaries or control. In addition to federal funding, villages may also receive public and private grants, loans and have business interests.

Village Councils, or their equivalent, may be the only forms of government in some rural or isolated regions.

Elders: Age and wisdom are revered by the majority of indigenous cultures of which I am aware, certainly those in the northern hemisphere of North America. Elder gatherings and organizations are seldom formal in the western way of doing things. However, they have exceptional power and respect within most aboriginal groups. Elders are the gatekeepers, historians and synthesizers of the native ways. Everything of importance will be run by them in one fashion or another and they will respond, or not, as they wish.

Intersections: These entities have varying interrelationships. They are likely to share board members, work in or with the other organizations, and have family or clan ties, and certainly know or know of each other. While each group may be fiercely independent of each other, they simultaneously need and desire to work together for mutual benefit.

Political Arms: In addition to individual avenues of preservation, there is often an umbrella organization, which presents native views to state, federal and local governments. In Alaska, this is often the Alaskan Federation of Natives (AFN), which acts as an advocate for Native issues of culture, land, economics, or any other important interest raised by its members.

Why would I want to be involved in a business relationship with Natives?

Ah-h-h! Herein lies the crux of the matter to profit maker! I hesitated long and hard in putting this as the first chapter in this book. My sense of caution didn't want the reader to be blinded by dollars without seeing the bigger picture of why money might not be sufficient reason alone to be doing business with Native people. It certainly won't be the best path to success in such a venture.

Nonetheless, money is a primary motivator, so read on…. but don't forget the rest of the book.

A Niche market? Maybe, but it is a substantial niche. In Alaska alone, for example, almost every village is a federally recognized tribe in itself, which makes for 229 individual tribes in one state alone[1] accounting for between 16% and 19% of the full State population and over 44,000,000 acres of owned land. Alaska is only fifth among States with large Native populations, preceded by Oklahoma, Arizona, California, and New Mexico[2].

The population of Native Americans and Alaskan Eskimos in the U.S. is 2.4 million[2], almost half of which are under 28 years old. They are 1.5% of the U.S. population[4] but growing at almost 1% per year, which makes them one of the faster growing groups in the country[2].

There are over 102,000 Native businesses in U.S., which increased a whopping 92% between 1987 and 1992 alone. That same period saw 102% increase in receipts from these businesses with over 8 billion dollars in revenues [2].

About $500 million federal dollars goes to Alaskan tribes each year[1].

Of First Nations in Canada, there are 600+ bands, which are funded at almost 6 billion dollars in Federal funds[5] [7]. First Nations people presently own 6.3% of Canadian Land[7] with another 15% under dispute via Supreme Court Rulings[8].

None of these numbers reflect income from alternative business activities like gaming, which brought in an additional 4.5 billion dollars in 1995 alone for Native Tribal entities.

Note: The events of September 11, 2001 caused a restriction and even shutdowns of many U.S. Federal websites. Consequently, current information access has become quite restrictive. The sites referenced are still online as of this printing and current information is available as public documents through regular government channels.

In Short: Native people operate in and around a vibrant economic system that is not necessarily easily visible. The partial list above totals over $19,000,000,000. It is a generally a young group with a substantial growth ratio[2]. It has taken a while for them to come up to speed during the cultural transitions but they have embraced commerce, under their own rules.

Applications: Good business opportunities exist in the Native world but Do Your Research!

Native people have become worldly and sharp business people with conservative views.

Native people have been taken advantage of and have long memories of what has been lost to them. Be prepared for strong and detailed negotiations and a lack of tolerance for B.S.

Deals will have to be considered 'fair' in many aspects that are not common in non-native interactions. Be prepared to respectfully consider whatever comes along.

Nothing that is of active negative concern to the Elders will move anywhere.

Be very careful with legalities. Most recognized Native entities have legal exceptions to a variety of laws and a strong inclination to protect hard-won rights.

See Also: Every other section in this book

PROTOCOL

"Ikt Kloshe Ooahut Wawa"

The Instructions of Ptahhotep, written in Egypt around 2500 B.C., advises "When sitting with one's superiors, laugh when they laugh."[1]

What exactly is protocol? We hear of it in terms of visiting heads of state and dignitaries. It has that exotic sense of foreign worlds and unusual habits, of strange smells, food and dress. In our world of alliances, coalitions and trade relations with nation-states of all stripes, we do seem to inherently understand the need to tread softly and attempt to both make others comfortable with us and to avoid offense.

Yet, within our own state and national borders, we often seem to feel this practice of respectful tolerance is unnecessary. North America likes to see itself as a melting pot, yet a stew seems to be a more appropriate metaphor. We seem to be lumps of various identities that meld, intermix and separate in a varied and constantly changing mix. A single protocol, or method of relating for these differing identities denies the existence of the very chasms we are attempting to bridge.

In the simplest form, protocol is simply good manners. Protocol is the base means by which we have productive interaction[2]. In order to not trip over our own feet, it is necessary to do a little preliminary research into exactly what constitutes proper behavior in any situation with which we are not already familiar.

Most of us inherently know to be more aware in dangerous situations, to watch our step on uneven ground, or to move slowly in dark strange rooms. Socially, we attempt to heighten our sensitivity in new relationships, in politically touchy situations and in any house or neighborhood where we sense that we don't fit well. Where we know that we don't know the rules of the road, we proceed with caution.

Indigenous cultures, groups, associations, societies, villages or individuals are a part of the North American world in which what we know, as compared to what we don't know, often puts us in very bad stead. What we know should more properly be stated as 'what we think we know' for the Native world is as different, interesting and exotic as any culture on earth – and older than most of them.

Our misconceptions honed by the propaganda of history and sold to us as entertainment by the media for generations, is why 'what we think we know' is our primary enemy. Learning what to do or say, how to act requires unlearning of what we started with 'knowing'.

Cultural awareness with the many ethnic and cultural groups scattered through our own society may be even more essential with Indigenous people. Native tribes in the U.S. are separate nations with history, government and social rules that were ancient when Rome was in power, before England existed, before most of the world's major religions were formulated.

When you do learn the proper protocols for visiting with Native groups, you will have touched the mists of time, and be transported to the very origins of your own humanity.

In Short: Assume that you know very little about the Aboriginal inhabitants of North America. The media images of Native life are exactly that – media images, feeding off of what sells.

There are hundreds of Aboriginal groups in North America, 'one size does not fit all'[2]. The range of consequences for violations of protocol throughout the world can range from the simple snicker to life threatening, depending on the situation.

Applications: Stop all assumption and do your preparatory work.
Find or hire a staff member or consultant with experience or a sensitive interest.
Consider cultural sensitivity training for all your staff – from top management down to line workers.
See also: Politeness, Power & Respect, Silence and Patience, Gifting, Language

A Gathering of the tribes in Juneau, AK.

Visiting Maori from New Zealand

WHAT IS CULTURE?
"Iktah Tumtum Tillikum?"

Freedom is limited. You can create an increasingly positive life for yourself and your people only if you understand and deal with the limits that life, and especially your culture, has been imposing on you and everyone else from the moment of conception. Culture shapes you, biases you toward certain goals, and permits you only a limited number of means to reach those goals. –J Bilocerkowycz.(3).

There are many attempts to adequately answer this question. Ultimately it is the totality of information presented to you by your social group. It is the conglomeration of rules, values, meanings, ways of thinking, and even options available provided by your family, spiritual teachings, community and significant others from conception onward. Culture, along with genetics, is the most enduring, powerful, and invisible shaper of our communication behavior.(1)

Not all of it is spoken and may not be easy to define even if one has grown up in it. Most cultural habits are not even conscious and quite likely very little of it is written down. Much of culture comes simply from modeling, from repetitive behaviors and actions of those around us. Precious little comes from books – far more comes from family stories, stories of the culture, of the dim past and other tales of yesterday, sitting around the campfire. The North is a place where you will often find yourself totally alone yet your very survival is often completely dependent on what has been shared in the company of family and friends.

There are many cultures in the North Country – each unique and yet each sharing some base commonalities. In most of western society, if there is any division it is commonly simplistic – Indians and Eskimo's. Indians received their label via Columbus' mistake and Eskimo is actually a Cree (Indian) word – both are considered derogatory terms (or, at least, impolite and uninformed) to many folks. Except for the student of or participant in such cultures, this is the big lump of western culture, of TV and novels; of childhood games – chunked down to the lowest common denominators and accepted as sufficient truth.

It is a surprise for many who come north, to find that there are myriads of widely different groups amid this simplistic and arbitrary, division. For the Eskimo-Aleut language group we are talking of the Chukchee, Inuit, Innu, Aleut, Yupik, Inupiat, Inuvialuit to name but a few. For Indians there are Athapaskan, Algonquin, Siouan, Iroquoian in large scale North American language divisions that further divide into Dene, Cree, Ojibwa, Slavey, Blackfoot, Blood, Dakota, Sarcee, Chipewayan, Micmacs and Mohawk to, again, only name a few.(Notes)

Each group is unique, with differing customs, language, history and appearance. Most groups living in harsh climates seem to have a hunter-gatherer heritage but many, in less harsh climates, have a long history of agriculture. In my experience, where these apparently disparate societies intersect is in their common reverence and understandings of relationship. Relationship is not simply the connection between two human beings but the various relationships between all things – and the appropriate balancing thereof.

We, in the western way of thinking, divide and separate issues. We compartmentalize and deal with one issue at a time. The Native _worldview_ and cultural training is _holistic_ and multi-tasked. The act of separating one portion out of the whole would serve to deny and disrespect the natural influences and results of that portion of the universe exerts and is exerted upon. The issue in relationships is balance and harmony, without which nothing lasting will occur.

In Short: Culture is that set of rules that you learned either by modeling and listening closely to your Elders or the rules that were learned by breaking them and suffering the results. Very few groups share an exact common culture although they may share commonalities. Protocols between groups or individuals are much more than just being 'nice' in the ways of your own world which may, in fact, even be offensive in another culture.

Applications: When you are going to interact with a group that you are personally unfamiliar with, find somebody who is knowledgeable if you wish to avoid the majority of the fatal _faux pas_.

Just because you may have historically lumped groups together (Indians, Eskimos, Latinos) it is a deadly way to start a business relationship with a single group. Each group, even within a larger group, will be different

All cultures have survival value, otherwise, they wouldn't exist. Take the time to find and acknowledge aspects of that culture that you personally appreciate. Find the commonalities, then learn about and negotiate through the differences.

See also: Who & Why, The Personal Connection, History

CONTACT

"Elip Chako Kunamokst"

"The voyage of discovery lies not in seeking new horizons, but in seeing with new eyes." - Marcel Proust

Many western people see the history of aboriginal groups as beginning with the time of contact with the west. Of course, in order to contact a civilization, it must be already in existence, so this might more properly be called the period of modern history. Contact, however defined, remains a poor concept or timeline for gauging the opportunity for cultures to begin to know and understand each other.

In North America, I believe that the majority of folks relate the contact period with their own regional history. On the east coast of the U.S. this might be 300+ years; in the Western U.S. 150-200 years. In the global world of mass communications, many folks believe that all cultures have had significant access to most of the high definition cultures of the major powers.

However, many Indigenous cultures have had considerably less exposure than is commonly held. In the first place, contact itself does not create significant understanding. A few of the Ahtna people of Interior Alaska had "contact" with a few Russian traders 125 years ago, and some gold rush miners passed through their region a little over a hundred years ago[1]. At the far outskirts of their territory, a massive mineral operation existed some eighty years ago but only affected a small portion of people at the extreme edges of their lands.

As trails became dirt roads, the occasional primitive travelers lodge, or trading post, was established by a few non-native people for business purposes – usually 35-70 miles apart. This did not occur until the 1900's-30's. World War II caused the largest and most regular influx of non-native incursions into the area and many of the troops developing the Alaska Highway and Alaska Communications system were southern Black soldiers[2][3], further confusing the issues for local people.

This timeline brings it down to only about 70 years since the bulk of Ahtna people have had significant contact with the western world. Many living Ahtna Elders can remember the first time they saw a white person in the flesh. Sixty years is but two full generations – a very short time to assimilate and understand a very different way of operating and thinking.

For many northern groups in Canada, significant contact timelines are often even more recent. Rupert Ross notes that initial, sustained 'contact' for many northern tribes is closer to 50 years[4:xxiii]. 50-60 years puts contact, and its accompanying social/political changes, within the lifetime of a single adult.

In Short: Native people, especially those in the far north, have had precious little time to absorb full understanding of a fundamentally different system. Adopting another system, in full, has little appeal while their own long-lived systems are so rich and vibrant. It is remarkable that they have been so willing to interact as much as they have.

Applications: Do your research before you make blanket statements. It won't matter if you are academically correct if you are culturally wrong.

Be careful to neither over nor underestimate the capabilities or experiences of the folks you are dealing with. There are wide ranges and many gaps in western thinking, but remember that Native groups have survived and succeeded in worlds you cannot imagine.

Understand that considerable cultural sensitivity is required in every aspect of an interface.

Find a local librarian and a range of local knowledgeable people to talk with. No one point of view is likely to give you what you need to know.

See Also: History, Personal Connection, Education

Kaskae

In the very old days, villages in interior Alaska were very small and wide spread. Many groups were little more than large families and marriage partners – often as few as 15 people. Alaska is tough – food occasionally comes in abundance but on a regular basis it is hard to come by.

Any stranger approaching an encampment was a possible threat. At the same time, rules of politeness, the yearning for news and the desire for positive alliances required some mode of both protecting and opening. When a stranger approached, most people hid, children were brought inside, men gathered their weapons nearby.

One person in the group, most probably an Elder but, in the Native way, it could have been anybody that functions as the kaskae. Like most Native words, kaskae can have many meanings from chief to powerful person to wise person or counselor. He/she was a person of respected skills. Essentially, the kaskae was a kind of informal camp boss when there wasn't anyone higher around.

Traditionally, the abode of the kaskae, had an animal skin hanging outside. This may seem a pretty stupid sign to most folks – didn't Indians always have skins and animal parts around? The reality is that many things were made of skins, in fact, every part of an animal. Consequently, it would have almost been an extravagance to waste one simply for a kind of decoration, a flag of sorts.

This symbol, among the Ahtna Athabascan, meant this was a safe house for a stranger to approach. Approaching this house was a kind of neutral zone. The resident of this home would talk with the stranger, finding out his clan and tribe, his family and relations and in general get a feel for the values carried by this person.

There was then a type of symbol that passed to the villagers on the level of care they needed to take with this person.

This protocol still exists in some rural villages among the Ahtna Athabascans. When, as the area mental health counselor, I came into a new village, I would visit first the matriarch and bring a small gift, as is the custom. We would usually share coffee or tea and visit for a spell. If I left the house with a smile and a wave, the village was essentially closed to me. If the good bye was a formal handshake out in public, I was acceptable to be in the village but with considerable caution. If I was hugged heartily, the village was open to me almost as if I were a relative.

HIGH CONTEXT SOCIETIES

"Kloshe Kopa Konaway Kumtucks"

The salvation of mankind lies only in making everything the concern of all. ~ Alexander Solzhenitsyn

It was the premier cultural anthropologist, Edward T. Hall, that first defined cultures as high and low context with their varying characteristics. As with anything else, the intensity of any particular culture will vary but one dominant indicator of rural and isolated cultures is that they tend to be high-context. The high and low context labels of cultures display a number of unique characteristics.

A low-context society – most Western societies – is marked by a discomfort with periods of silence and uses constant conversation and many words for descriptions and explanations. Most of us live in high density populations where one person only knows about a relatively few others and, in meeting a wide range of people of varying backgrounds and experiences, it is imperative to provide and receive information about each other in order to interact effectively[1]. Much of the knowledge is codified, public, and external. Most meetings are task oriented with activities and decisions revolving around what needs to be done and who will be responsible for accomplishing them.

In high-context societies, silence and observation are the more normal mode of interaction[2:13]. Most members are fully familiar with the same cultural history and local knowledge. There is simply no reason to reiterate what is commonly known and shared [1]. Relationships between people tend to be dense, intersecting and long-term in familial, clan and tribal groupings. In the same vein, these societies tend to be holistic in thought patterning – inherently understanding the big picture of the situation – its ripples and permutations in a social context, because of a common background. Knowledge is personal and interpersonal. Most interactions are primarily relational and interpersonal.

The only analogy I can immediately provide is to imagine that you are on an extended camping trip – a yearlong camping trip in a remote region. Picture your group consisting of 10-30 people, mostly related to you in some fashion and of varying ages. Let's assume also that you know of 10 or more groups like yours somewhere in the same environment and that, also like you, they are wholly dependent upon each other for their individual survival – food, shelter and protection. Like you, they only have each other to talk to, learn from and depend on every day of their life.

Once a year, you come together with some or all of these groups – perhaps at a favored fishing location. For a week or two, you socialize, talk, and listen to the experiences of the other. You make music, dance, prepare food and generally have a good time. Then, for the next 50 weeks you return to your usual group and situation.

Think you might know most things about your cohorts – their likes and dislikes, their desires and dreams, their skills and abilities, their religious beliefs and histories? Now, extend that picture for one lifetime, then a couple of centuries, and then thousands of years.

In Short: High context societies share more than merely a lifetime together but are intricately and intimately interwoven with a common history that stretches for millennia. In-group and out-group definitions are clear and distinct.

Applications: Understand that the verbal, _gestural_ and nonverbal clues you usually count on to gauge the effect or level of comprehension that your presentation is receiving will likely be simply 'not there' and/or easily misinterpreted. By the same point, your exhibition and characteristics are likely going to be interpreted commonly by the group cultural interpretations.

Silence from the audience should not to be interpreted as rejection but continually filling in the silences will be considered as confusing and not giving people time to think.

Working one faction against another faction is likely to be much more complex than you expect and the probability is that the results will be negative. Given a conflict like that in your world, where would your loyalties lie – with those you know or those you don't know?

See also: <u>Non-Interference</u>, <u>Family</u>, <u>Silence</u>, <u>Non-Verbal</u>

THE PERSONAL CONNECTION

"Skookum Sikhs"

Friendship is to be purchased only by friendship. A man may have authority over others, but he can never have their hearts but by giving his own. ~ Thomas Wilson

In old times, in central Alaskan *Athabascan* communities, there was a position known as the Kaskae[1][4]. There are a variety of definitions for the Kaskae (Qeshqa in Dena'ina)[5], from chief to counselor, or respected person, but those so designated were often the one household in the village where a stranger was allowed to safely go first. The Kaskae would then talk with the person, perhaps questioning relations and values, often just sensing intent[1]. The particular way in which the person left that particular household (accompanied, or not, to the door vs. hugged vs. handshakes) was a type of code that let the other villagers know the level of openness or trust to provide this visitor[1][2][3].

With the advent of large-scale intercultural interactions, this particular position may not exist any longer. However, the characteristics of a tightly interwoven society continue with its common understandings and interconnected dependencies. It is necessary to have a personal relationship with one or more individuals in the community. With and through this person, you will be allowed access to other aspects of village life and will be guided to the places and people you need to be talking to.

Depending upon the social structure of the community or organization, people may be related by family, clan, village, tribe and/or region as well as politics and *propinquity*. It is not likely that you will find your way around by simple genealogical or organizational charts.

Although usually having access to the latest electronic and office equipment, palm pilots and PC's, these are essentially conservative societies, trusting in each other and in known personal relationships. There can be investment in image and competence in the newest ideas and methodologies but, in a sense of balance, the new must mesh with the old in some acceptable fashion and that fashion will always be related to a cultural familiarity and to the thoughts of related others.

In addition to access, the personal connection will prepare you on how to act & present properly as well as teach you, mostly by modeling, what to avoid in circumstances where the damage cannot be repaired relatively easily. If you know one person, and you know this person in the context of being a real person yourself, you will soon know many more members of the community.

In this way, the person you are and the project you represent will be represented in the community long before you actually schedule your presentation.

In Short: Trust and value are based on interpersonal contact and relationships, not on academic or business acumen. The time spent on developing personal relationships will forecast the success of your project.

Applications: Emails and faxes are no way to start a relationship with a Native group. Send a representative specifically to be introduced to and to meet local people who can help with your needs.

Once you do have relationships within the organization or the community, retain the same people for all negotiations and representational occasions.

Be observant – in the Native way, learning is provided by observation. You will not be given a handbook. Much will be decided, not by intensity but by perceived intent. If the intent is respectful, you will likely be seen as worth teaching further.

See also: Dress, Gifting, Politeness, Silence Smell, Elders, Time

Blankets: Sockeye salmon, filleted, cut and being smoked for the winter

Moosehide: Fleshed, stretched and drying to be used for making drums

HISTORY, WHOSE?

"Hyas Ahnkuttie Yiem"

"...all this time thousands of years, Indians look up and think that it is K'elt'aeni -- hundreds of generations of our forefathers look up and think it Mount K'elt'aeni; but Indians not very smart. First white man come along ten years ago, he say Ah, Hah, Mount Sanford... and Mount Sanford it is today, my people". Sanford Nicolai, at potlatch[8].

I am here reminded of bringing a group of Elders to conference with a School Superintendent about problems with the children. The Superintendent went on and on about the state of his knowledge, degrees, technological superiority and the 300 year unprecedented successful history of the United States. Under whelmed by his tirade, one of the Elders quietly said, "We understand that you are new at these things".

To the Elders, this was merely a statement of fact and sympathy, an offer to help and open up the discussion to mutual interaction. To the Superintendent, it was an affront and a challenge. He dismissed the meeting.

Whose history and which history would really be the pertinent questions to entertain. History, as written in western textbooks is only that view of the past as seen through the lenses of prejudices, opinions, sources and knowledge of the author and buffeted by the costs of production and distribution while withstanding the influences of powerful others who think differently.

Anthropologists and archeologists can date the existence of North American Indigenous people for 7-12,000 years, positing various theories of how they arrived[7]. Newer DNA research and archeological works suggest that 18,000+ years is more accurate[2][11][12]. Most Native groups own history says that they were always here[3], that they originated in the land they occupy. The nature of hunter-gatherer lifestyles finds gathering of material goods nonfunctional and builds few monuments of lasting materials. Even so, the physical record for 12 or so millennium is quite strong. The oral history is stronger yet.

Think about 12,000 – 35,000 years and a society that could and did pass its history, lessons on behavior, skills, mental maps, environmental information and rules of conduct on for countless generations. Check out the beginnings of Rome (753BC), China (2200BC), Egypt (5500BC) at those dates and you will find precious little.

In the realities of Western science, in the Human Genome Project, it is clear that we all have a common ancestry in time. The DNA evidence for the migration out of Africa occurred between 38,500 and 50,000 years ago[4][5][6]. The population of Europe by modern man is said to have occurred beginning 30,000 years ago[6][9][10]. The populating of North America also began about 30,000 years ago.

By 1500AD, the population of Europe was close to 80 million people. At 1500 in the America's, the population was between 40 and 140 million people depending on which researcher you believe[13][14]. In reality, _Europe and North America began as contemporaries and appear to have started out of the same base stock_. The only real difference is that in Europe, it was necessary to displace the previous wave of _Paleolithic_ occupants (Neanderthals) while there is little history of a significant previous population in the Americas.

If this scientific evidence remains validated, then we know three things. The first thing we know is that no individual is less evolved than any other, but our histories have taken different paths. _Aristotelian logic_ (3rd century BC) and the laws of _Hammurabi_ (1792-1750 BC) did not exist in the native path but equal understandings of the universe and social relationships did and that knowledge continues to serve them today.

The second thing that we know is that if those numbers are even close, it is no wonder there are differences in understanding and quite remarkable that the two groups coexist as well as they do.

Third, when we are dealing with the indigenous populations of North America, we may be dealing with the most ancient, continuous civilization on planet Earth. As such, we may be dealing with a _cosmology_, a worldview that is more direct to our human roots than any other such system in existence.

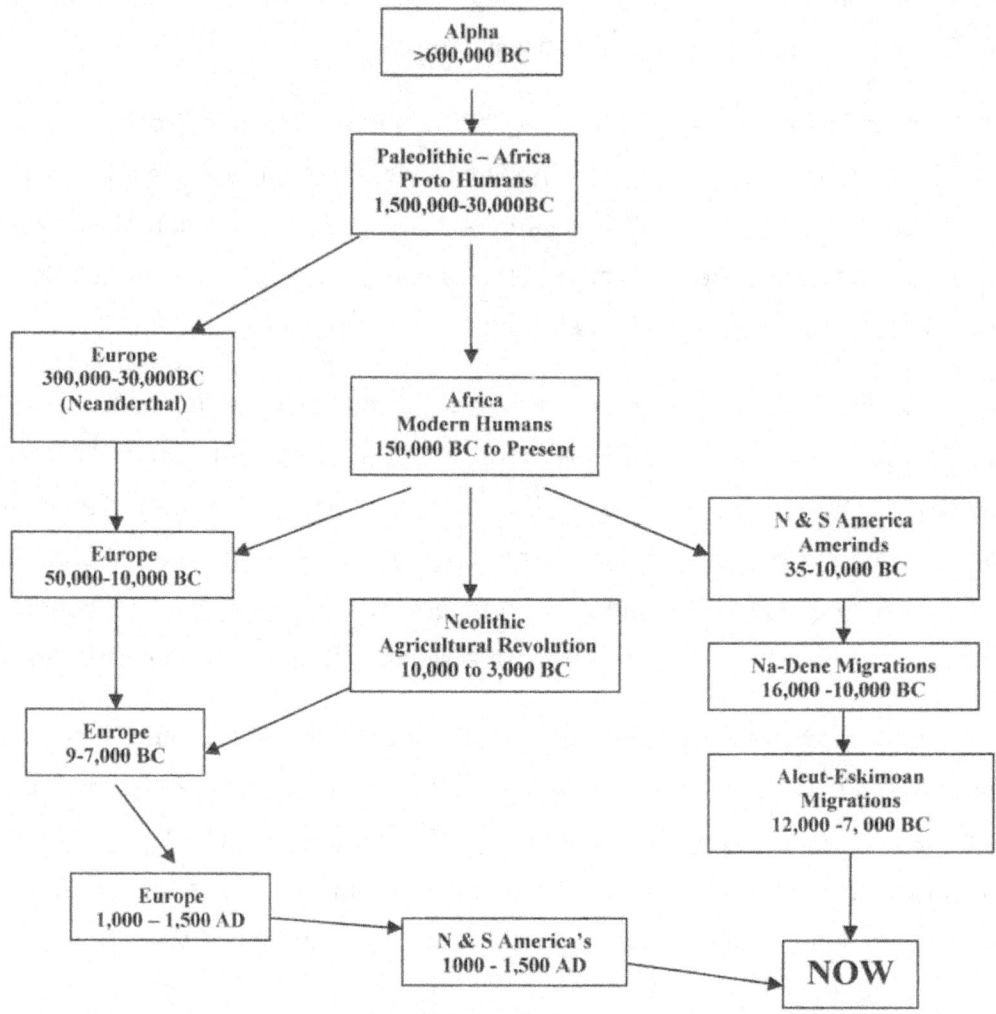

Figure 1. Comparative Migration Patterns

Fig. 1: The very broad diagram of human migration patterns relating to both Europe and the America's can bring up some subjective projections for cultural differences. Europe had a considerable mixing of, and competition between cultures for many centuries.   The Agricultural Revolution with its land based economy, structures of private property, ownership, laws, taxation, ruling structures and philosophies had over 8,000 years to solidify previous to contact with the Indigenous populations of the America's.

The New World, however, had a much larger land base to support its population growth with relatively little physical or philosophical competition. The worldview of the Aboriginal American had the opportunity to remain comparatively contiguous with its early beginnings. Successive migrations, until the European, had a similar journey through Asia and comparable origins.

If perseverance of a culture and a society over time is any indicator of the value of its knowledge, then the native cultures deserve our awe. They are not only ancient civilizations but they are survivor civilizations.

In Short: As far as I can ascertain, these cultures predate western society by several to many millennium. They were successful in their milieu for tens of thousands of years before Rome was started. Your first thought must be, "They are success stories!" What could there be of such great value that these cultures stand so strongly in the face of overwhelming physical, environmental, political and economic odds?

Applications: The perspective of most aboriginal people is long-term. Rushing them will only result in stonewalling which defeats the purposes of both parties. .

Put away your present assumptions and images provided by Zane Gray novels. The reality is much more interesting and much less divisive.

What you know can be of great value; what you don't know (but think that you do know) is what will get you in trouble. Enter the aboriginal world as a learner and an observer - you will find teachers.

See also: Contact, Education

CONSENSUS
"Tumtum Kunamoks"

They began their journey to today not where we did, with the Mediterranean world-view classically enunciated by Plato and Aristotle. They began it in Asia, then brought that Asian world-view to the reality of a harsh, nomadic existence on this land mass many thousands of years before Plato was born. They developed, refined and sustained it over those centuries, and it sustained them. **Rupert Ross, 1992. Dancing with a Ghost, p. xxii.**

Usually, western business people have a most difficult time with the indigenous concept of _consensus_. It simply flies in the face of western business training. For those who have endured or relished in debates, conflict negotiation, bidding wars, and generally aggressive win/lose dichotomy of the western world, the concept of consensus will be one of your biggest challenges.

Consensus is the standard of operation for most small tribes and villages(1:65). Even many of the corporate entities reflecting indigenous groups have a strong pressure to move along by consensus, usually overwhelming consensus. In your business negotiations, you may be primarily working with one person or department but a much larger entourage will make the final decision. Simply put, everybody must agree.

The cultural context of eons of isolated rural existence and coexistence has fomented a necessity for getting along. Mutual respect, tolerance and non-interference are hallmarks of indigenous cosmology. There are lifelong and historical cultural values of interdependence and sharing for survival and business is no different. Discussions will continue, formally and informally, until the vast majority of the major participants agree or an active decision will not arrive.

The dissenter or dissenters will not necessarily be identified, as this would violate the basic rule of non-interference and cause inappropriate public focus on an individual who was merely expressing their opinion. While there will certainly be differences of opinions in the decision making process, the process itself is not adversarial. It is more common that there will not even be a decision to <u>not</u> go forward with a project or deal – it will merely be avoided until it goes away of its own accord. This too reflects the native preference for non-confrontation and saving face for both sides.

For most Westerners, the lack of a united front indicates a lack of focus or control. They see the need for consensus (and the common difficulty of attaining it) as discord, conflict and the inability to cooperate. In the Aboriginal worldview, the lack of consensus is a prime example of cooperative agreement – an agreement to not go forward in respect of the understanding that the opinions/knowledge of others is sacrosanct also. A lack of consensus is a respectful 'no' vote.

For the most part, those in the Native world and in the positions to make decisions must make only decisions that are acceptable to the vast majority of their constituents. The various boards of directors and councils are usually actively involved and are made up of a wide range of representatives who may also be family or political leaders. Indigenous histories and stories are replete with lessons of actions where a non-conservative approach, one made without proper consultation, lead to undesirable outcomes. The values intertwined with the decisions to be made include respect and appreciation for each individual member and their way of looking at things.

In Short: Native peoples have the usual range of all beings – there are those who are honest and those who are greedy, some aggressive and some reticent, there are weak ones and strong ones. Each of these folks is highly likely to know the strengths and foibles of the others. How you deal with all of these will be reflected in their evaluation of you, which will, in the end, be more important than whatever you are presenting.

In reaching decisions, each will attempt to fully accommodate the beliefs or wishes of the others, even if it means changing their own.

Application: Leave yourself a relatively open timeline.

Pushing will only meet resistance and is counter productive.

Ask for concerns and try to plan your project and presentation with all of them in mind. Address all issues.

See also: Non-interference, Family, Silence & Patience, Time, Elders

CULTURAL AND INTELLECTUAL PROPERTY

"Nika Tillikum, Nika Tumtum, Nika La Lang"

Property is more than the thing which a person owns. It is elementary that it includes the right to acquire, use, and dispose of it. The Constitution protects these essential attributes of property .... There can be conception of property aside from its control and use, and upon its use depends its value. - Buchanan v. Warley (Supreme Court decision, 1917)

There is considerable sensitivity and conflict in Indigenous communities over the issues of cultural and intellectual property rights. Cultural property would be identified as social, artistic and ceremonial activities common to the group such as dances, clothing, stories, belief systems and ceremonies. Intellectual property includes *traditional* knowledge (environmental, scientific etc.) and the techniques or uses for items or materials.

Because of the basic value of sharing, many aboriginal people have seen their knowledge and customs usurped with neither adequate permission nor compensation. This remains a thorny problem due to differences in the concept of ownership between collective societies and western legal frameworks.

When a Native person tells a traditional story, you will notice that the story telling includes where that person learned the story and even farther back, as far back as the teller knows. In western words, it is accredited. This validates the story and helps insure accuracy as others may know or can check on its veracity. The accreditation then becomes an additional value within the values identified by the story itself. Taken out of context, the story itself loses its potency as a learning tool.

The case is similar with other intellectual properties. Traditional Indigenous knowledge is ancient, complex and wide-ranging. One person or another may be the community 'expert' on a particular area but the overall ethos is that the survival of the individual is dependent upon the survival of the community and vice-versa. These insights and understandings are shared throughout the community.

A single piece of traditional knowledge may be the result of literally eons of conception, experimentation and refinement. It may be applicable to one place or one set of circumstances or it may apply across the planet. Many of the medicines still in use and foods that end up on your table may have originated with this very process and these very cultures[4].

Collective ownership is not recognized under many western laws, which identify an individual or individuals as originators and, consequently, owners of concepts, ideas, processes and products[1:8]. In collective societies, many things belong to a family, a clan or the entire tribe. These laws are under the process of change as many legal scholars and organizations recognize the validity of Native claims in these areas.[1][2][3]

In most indigenous societies, ownership of other than personal items belongs to the group. Concurrently, speaking for the group is a serious task – one only undertaken with considerable consultation, discussion and permission from the group itself.

In Short: What you see, hear or understand by participation in any activities is a privilege. Knowledge is not to be considered ownership. Many ceremonies, dances, designs, songs and stories contain historical, spiritual and family attachments – to copy or use them out of context and without permission is often considered theft.

Applications: Seek permission before publishing anything about the group with whom you are involved. Consider or discuss the use of 'release forms' that define how any knowledge will be used and compensated for.

Do not use the names of individuals, societies, tribes or anything similar in public pronouncements without specific written permission. Never use the names of the dead.

Take no pictures or use any kind of recording device without specific permission obtained in advance.

For business purposes, it doesn't matter whether the law is on your side if you misappropriate cultural properties. You may win the legal battle but will lose the business relationship.

See also: <u>Appendix A, #9 , Guidelines for Respecting Cultural Knowledge</u>

Engee'

"Engee'" has different names in different languages but all languages have a word with the same meaning. I learned "engee" as a word used by interior Athabascans of Alaska and it may have different names among different tribes even there, but every tribe has a word like it.

I mention it because the results of invoking 'engee' brings all sorts of approach and avoidance for non-natives – by its very nature it excites curiosity, creates assumption and frustrates learning. I would dare say that the mishandling of this specific interaction alone has done the largest damage between the cultures in that it becomes the basis for such baseless descriptions as 'superstitious, mythical, secretive and even stupid'.

Engee' means 'forbidden'. It simply means something that is not to be talked about. Many things may be engee' – religious beliefs, behaviors, foods, thoughts, animals, clothing, and even people. Native people have complex rules of behavior that have important affect for both individuals and tribes.

The first question in every white persons mind is "Why is it forbidden?" and the second question is "How do you know it is forbidden if you can't talk about it?"

The likely response that will come from these two questions is uncomfortable silence and avoidance. This is neither because it is truly forbidden by some power that can't be crossed nor is it necessarily because the person really doesn't know. In truth, we all learn things from those around us as we grow up that are not necessarily put into words – food preferences, how the parents feel about some other individual or race, even proper ways to dress but that is seldom the reason for the answer 'engee'.

More properly, 'engee' means 'sensitive' which further means that it is only to be discussed with a certain level of trusted individuals. Just as within your own culture, there are subjects and matters that are more properly discussed with intimates, parents, physicians, religious confidants, or authorities, not everything is open for general discussion. One of the rules of polite conversation in the western world is the avoidance of discussion about politics, sexuality or religion according to 'Dear Abby' and 'Miss Manners'.

Rather than take offense or to push beyond appropriate limits, it is more practical to understand the reply of engee to mean that 'we are not at that level in our relationship to discuss this kind of matter'. It is simply a matter of politeness. When you get to that level, with the appropriate person, those understandings will be given willingly.

DRESS

"Iktas"

Those who make their dress a principal part of themselves, will, in general, become of no more value than their dress. - William Hazlitt

Oh, yes – that dark, solid-blue "power suit". It had to be earned and it was expensive but the rewards seem obvious. Along with the rest of the presentation, it has the power to beguile, threaten, intimidate and exude confidence, authority, dominance[1] and success. Throw in the proper posture and grooming, add the Rolex and the fine Cuban cigar, tip the chin up for an air of diffidence and the picture is complete. It is meant to portray power and success – a show of difference, and it works.

Sometimes and in some places.

On the wrong person or in the wrong setting, it can give the presentation of ostentation and sham, of glitter without gold – a hierarchical power play not fully deserved – a separation not desirable. Military uniforms and men's suits have long been understood in the study of non-verbal behavior as unmistakable statements of being closed off [1]. Presenting so protectively indicates at least unilateral distrust.

Most Indigenous people have a long and painful history of being dominated by other cultures and, they have immediate defenses and strong reactions – negative reactions.

I have, in my possession, a potlatch item that was given in honor many years ago. It is a beautiful hair-bone choker necklace with an ornate, beaded rendition of a 'white man's" tie backed by moose hide. It was given to the headman of an Athabascan village both to denote honor and to allow him to deal with the dominant culture on an even basis. The key word here is 'even'.

The worldview of most Native cultures is based on respect – mutual respect. Respect is based on what you have done – for others, not for yourself. It is based on skills, deeds and wisdom, which have benefited the community. The 'Chief' or whatever the title given by a particular community or band is not the C.E.O of the Western style of business. It is an honor title that carries little direct power but great responsibility, for it is most often an egalitarian society where each can contribute or not on a voluntary basis.

This is not to say that Native people do not like nice things or that there are not differences in finances or whose word carries more or less strength. It is meant to convey that respect is earned and does not come automatically with position or self-portrayals.

In Short: Native people come in every stripe and level of wealth and/or sophistication. In their normal lives, they are seldom image conscious and are suspect of those who are. Your quality of character and sense of respect will be your avenue within this culture. Don't rely on external imagery for favorable reactions to your icons of power and success.

Applications: Many, if not most, village councils and similar indigenous governing bodies are voluntary, non-paying positions. Meetings are often held in the evenings so as not to interrupt the workday and people usually come in their normal, everyday clothes.

"When in Rome, do as the Romans do…" is a phrase attributed to St. Ambrose (c. 350-397) and has been good advice for most of 2,000 years. Take the time to do some research – arriving in the area a day early is always a good move for a variety of information gathering activities. Be prepared to dress business-casual or working-casual in the conservative sense. A tie, for men, should only be considered as a sign of respect depending upon the formality of the occasion.

Depending on the length of your stay and relationships you are making, it would serve you well to have at least one set of outdoor work clothes appropriate for the region. It is useful to present yourself as a person who appreciates different aspects of life.

When entering an indigenous world, remember that for the most part, the preceding century(s) have been constant conflict with dominating or colonizing cultures. To avoid being seen as one of 'them', with the attached emotional and memory connotations, it is important to present as one of 'we'. I am not suggesting fakery, as these are very perceptive people, but rather to look closely at yourself and think before you do anything.

Do not attempt to incorporate your vision of a traditional Native article of clothing or adornment unless you are willing to answer a lot of questions that may make you look foolish.

See also: Cultural & Intellectual Property, Observation

EDUCATION

"Mamook Kumtuks"

I have never let my schooling interfere with my education. Mark Twain (1835-1910)

Formal (school) education, especially the trappings and attitudes thereof, can be a very sore point with many Aboriginal people. The range of formal, western education among them can range from almost none to end degrees from prestigious institutions and world-renowned expertise. A thoughtful and inner-directed culture, though, has not skimped on experiential and practical educations of the natural and spiritual worlds.

In living history, there is a strong and negative memory of forced removal from their families and homes to attend government required residential schools. As recently as the 1950's in the U.S. and as late as 1984 in Canada, children were forcibly taken to distant places that contain terrible memories of physical, cultural, sexual and emotional abuse[1][2]. The damage these schools caused to Native cultures is immeasurable and reverberates still.

This wide range of knowledge in varying dimensions within any community creates a formidable façade for the western businessperson to approach. While some individuals may not have high levels of formal education, they are none the less well educated and experienced in practical and traditional ways which have provided survival under conditions you may not be able to imagine. In terms of observation and intuitive skills, in relationships and values, they are lifelong learners. Additionally, there are usually many well-informed, astute, and educated persons within their tribal relations that will have input in the process.

In more rural and isolated areas, it is historically common for women to have attained the most formal education and to be in the positions that need that aspect of training. In rural populations, and considering the relative newness of interaction with western society, men tended to leave school earlier to pursue traditional roles as providers. Women, whose cultural and social roles often required staying close to home, also stayed longer in schools.

This is rapidly changing but some changes just aren't so rapid in the bush.

In short: Learning and knowledge are highly respected in the indigenous community – it is a path to survival and to wisdom. That said, formal learning, degrees and certificates are only as valuable as they are positively useful and not considered all that impressive. Remember also that perception is not necessarily reality.

Applications: The challenge of respect to all parties requires fluid and well-thought strategies.

Presentations should provide written specifics in clear, simple language as handout material but use graphs and other visuals(3:44) in actual meetings unless requested otherwise.

Never 'talk down' to an audience. What you think you see or know about someone may be far a field of your expectations.

Nuances of disrespect or superiority will be quickly noticed and repeatedly discussed.

Always take time to seek out questions or thoughts from your audience at regular intervals. Remember time considerations for all involved.

Offer to come back for further interaction if the meeting is running long rather than rush through things or be the cause of terminal boredom.

See also: <u>History</u>, <u>Silence</u>, <u>Politeness</u>

FAMILY

"Nika Tillikum"

"The bond that links your true family is not one of blood, but of respect and joy in each other's life." - Richard Bach

Despite the forced mixing of disparate groups by the creation of reservations, reserves and economic zones, family remains the absolute mainstay of Native relations. Family, in the Native way, is extended, complex and interrelated with many other aspects of Aboriginal society.

As mentioned in other chapters, a genealogical approach is not likely to be able to tell you family connections very easily. During my early days in Alaska, I had three offices with walls covered by butcher paper, trying desperately to visually know who was related to whom.   The first piece of useful knowledge came when I finally understood that 'Auntie' did not necessarily represent a parent's female siblings. It also does not exclude them. An 'Auntie' can be a title of endearment for any female who is nurturing, supportive, protective and/or wise for whom the speaker has affection and respect.

Many lines are *matrilineal* or follow the mother's lines; others are *patrilineal*. Many are *matriarchal*[2:81]. Women have seldom been excluded from any facet of native life. Historically, you may find individuals of either sex as chief, warriors and occasionally, hunters. Names may be changed at different stages in life. Marital relationships dissolve and are reformed. There may be birth names, childhood names, culturally based names and English names. Out of wedlock births are well tolerated and given support by the community. The fact that this confuses non-natives doesn't bother anybody a bit – they know who they are.

The family is the ultimate base unit of the Native community. Family has historically been related to physical survival, economic survival and political power and is the most important loyalty base. At one workshop exercise, the participants were asked to count the number of family members they could think of. Most non-natives in the group averaged about 30 people – most Native people were on their fifth or sixth pages and had just begun.

This is not meant to imply that any given family is a uniform, cookie-cutter entity. In fact, herein lies the basis of individuality and equality. Children are rarely disciplined in a physical sense or even spoken harshly to[1:68]. They are expected to learn by watching and at their own pace, in their own way, when the time is right. Bad behavior is seen, for the most part, as incomplete learning that will right itself in time with proper guidance and modeling. Much of what is seen as a lack of caring by the western observer is seen as respect for the individual in the Native way – even if the possible consequences are harsh. When children in groups cause interference with adult activities, the group as a whole is held accountable rather than the assignment of individual blame[1:66]. This is another reinforcement of solidarity with and responsibility to the group as a consistent value.

Children are included in the overall world of the family and the community almost immediately and infants are seldom put into a separate or quiet room. Immediately they are part of the group and observation/watching is the primary learning technique[1:63] [3:152]. Children are held and touched a great deal by many members of the group but there is little in the mode of specific expression of affection. The specific actions of the hugging, kissing, baby talk, cooing is relatively absent compared to Western habits. Physical contact in calm certainty is held in higher regard than intensified emotional contact[ibid]. Belonging is inherent in the structure and values of the family and tribal groups, reinforced from many and constant aspects of daily life[3:151].

At a toddler age, children are expected to be able to sit quietly for hours in the presence of adults. By the ages of eight or ten, children are often so self sufficient that they care for families, hunt independently, carry significant responsibility and do not need to directly inform adults of their constant whereabouts (1:67-8). (3:154).

There is little gender gap in the Native world. Husbands and wives, sons and daughters are seen as equivalent beings, equally entitled to knowledge, respect and freedom. It may appear otherwise, looking through western eyes and, as each couple are individuals, they may decide on a particular methodology of being a family. Often, those groups with more intermixing with non-native culture have a combination of western and native ways, for both good and bad.

The parts of Native families that resemble a hierarchy are respect based. Certainly every child needs a protector and provider until he or she can provide on its own. The difference in Native communities is that ability is not restricted to a certain age, size or gender. Persons are respected based on their knowledge and, more importantly, their wisdom.

Elders are the repositories of the largest storehouse of traditional, cultural and historical knowledge. It is their guidance and perspective, which is revered, not simply their age.

In Short: Within tribes, one family or another may hold the reigns of power – either historically, traditionally or momentarily. However, power is distributed in many ways within the group. Almost every decision will have a heavy family base.

Child rearing practices mirror the expectations of adult behavior and values. Self-discipline and self-control begin at the earliest ages. Group responsibility governs much of peer-to-peer activity

Applications: It is not valuable to align yourself with a single leader or family. Power distribution within Native cultures is not easily perceived or understood by the outsider.

Kinship titles (Auntie, Cousin) are used more commonly than names in conversations. Because the group is 'high context', these identities are known internally. The visitor must obtain clarity as to who is being referred to in order to become part of the conversation.

Visual learning as the primary learning modality begins almost at birth as does group identification. Consider this in training and apprenticeship programs.

See also: Elders, Non-interference, Power & Respect, Non-verbal, Silence, Appendix #10 Guidelines for Nurturing Culturally Healthy Youth

Tlingit Bear Clan Hat

Tlingit Eagle Clan Hat

Tlingit Frog Clan Hats

Tlingit Raven Clan Hat

CLANS, PHATRIES AND MOIETIES

"Sit'kum La lang"

Society is joint action and cooperation in which each participant sees the other partner's success as a means for the attainment of his own. - Ludwig von Mises

One of the early *potlatch* ceremonies that I was privy to in the Copper River region of Alaska involved a relatively poor family grieving the loss of a young family member. Potlatches can be very expensive ceremonies as the host family is responsible for feeding, housing and gifting many members of extended family, neighbors and countless other relations for 3 days. This particular potlatch saw the arrival of over two hundred fifty people into a village with a population of about fifty.

I couldn't figure out where a family that couldn't afford to get their truck fixed would find the significant funds to provide for such an event on relatively short notice. One evening I had the opportunity to ask this question of an Elder who was helping to guide me through my introduction to the area. The response was that extended *clan* members from around the territory donated many of the gifts. Although these were 'donations', there was a moral responsibility to return the favor in the future when the situation arose again.

In addition to family, tribal and business associations, many tribal groups have a *clan* system. This system of associations is often based on distant ancestry that creates a relationship that is not buffeted by generational changes within individual families.

Each tribal member belonged to a clan as well as having blood family relationships. Clan membership evolved as a group of people who traced their descent from a common, but often, mythical source[2] [5] [6] [7] – perhaps a cultural icon too far back in time to create a clear, direct relationship. Often the clan maintained a symbol, perhaps an animal whose characteristics clan members identified with, attempted to emulate and used the emblem of this animal as its totem (3) (5) (6) (7). Membership, depending on the individual tribe, would descend from the clan of the father or of the mother (2).

"These clans were also exogamous-meaning that individuals could not marry another member of the same clan(7). Thus, a man of the Wolf clan, for example, was required to marry a woman from a different clan, but their children would belong to the Wolf clan. The wolf clan children of this marriage were of a different clan than children born of their father's sister or their mother's brother's marriage, and cousins of that type-called cross cousins-were considered suitable or even ideal marriage partners. Marriage was prohibited with one's parallel cousins: the children of one's father's brother or mother's sister" (2).

Clans were often grouped into phatries, which were a cooperative assembly of similarly related clans. This assembly of clans was also exogamous in that one could not marry a person whose clan was of the same *phatry*, or grouping of clans. Members of the same phratry had obligations of providing one another with hospitality and mutual assistance. (2) (5) (6) (7).

If there are only two groupings of phatries, the term then changes to moieties (5)(7). A *moiety* can consist of two clans or two groups of clans (phatries) so that the society always retains a balance of opposition(6).

Before the advent of modern styles of government, clans had individual traditional responsibilities for various aspects of social order, such as leaders, diplomats, peacemakers, warriors, protectors and spiritual or health providers within the tribe (1) (2).

Clans, unlike bands and local groups, are not family, spatially, or politically defined and create networks of relations that extend beyond individual bands. "Clan relationships provided bonds with distant groups, enhancing cohesion for the larger groups and promoting peaceful relations"[4].

The greatest similarity in Western society, that I am able to relate to, might be a fraternal society or a sorority with the exception that membership is not voluntary with Clans, as you are born into them. Clans provided defined leadership the various arenas of social need and were a major part of the organized governmental structure of the time.

Today, many traditional clan systems are in disarray and the original force and power of clans is diminishing with proceeding generations. Modern forms of government have duplicated most of their functions and the cash based society has blunted many of their activities.

None the less, they still exist and still function in many places that I am familiar with – often very quietly among elder members of the tribes. As with semi-secret societies in all cultures, clans may see a resurgence as the need arises or as cultural identities re-strengthen.

In Short: Clans are a grouping relationship of people that is not developed out of family relationships, political persuasions or even local tribal affiliations. Clans have had, and often still have traditional functions within tribes.

Without being a full member of a particular culture, one cannot say with certainty whether clans are functioning or not, or to what extent. It is not something that it is acceptable to discuss with anyone other than another clan member.

However, it is yet another example of relationships within a culture that can effect relations between cultures and are part of the mindset of individual values, apart from official position.

Applications: This is another example of non-obvious relationships within Native cultures. It is also another reason not to assume that you have a lock on who is on what side of any issue.

The complexity of relationships in Native cultures is reason enough to avoid any improprieties or the patronage of what appear to be internal rivalries.

See also: Family, Elders, Patronage, High Context Society, Who & Why

GIFTING

"Potlatch"

We make a living by what we get, but we make a life by what we give. — Winston Churchill

Gift giving is a standing tradition in the indigenous world. It is both a consideration of good manners and a sign of respect and caring. In many Athabascan potlatch traditions, it can take on massive and complex proportions.

In its simplest form, potlatch is a celebration ceremony that, over history, has been used to mark many occasions. My own experience with potlatch has been almost entirely involved with periods of grief and death. The final day of the potlatch ceremony, gifts are given – often to each of the attendees, but not necessarily for the same reasons. Gifts may be given for services provided to the deceased in his/her lifetime or to the family in their time of need. Gifts are also given to emphasize the family or clan connections, responsibilities or historical debts to others. Gifts may be given simply as political expediencies and reminders.

The giving of gifts on such occasions also has multiple layers of meaning. The ceremony itself honors the departed family member, identifies the status of the givers, redistributes wealth in the community, re-establishes traditions, confirms relationships, reinforces the values of sharing, brings the extended community together and aids in the healing process.

The giving or receipt of a gift, however, has no strings attached. The gift itself is transferred ownership from one person to another. Once given, there are no rules, spoken or implied, about what the new owner is allowed to do with that gift. Many is the time I have seen a substantial gift such as a rifle be immediately traded or sold before the ceremony was over.

In the western world, this would cause many a bent nose and disrupted relationship. For, in the Western world, the gift itself carries importance. In the Native world, it is the act of giving and the recognition that are of the most importance – the object itself is merely a symbol that represents the meaning. In the Native world, the symbol is transient, the value is in the recognition of the relationship.

For the most part, the gifts are practical – guns for hunting, blankets for warmth, crafts for use or wearing. I have seen songs created and given in potlatches and even money. The cash, like the other gifts, is not a repayment for expenses incurred but again, a symbol that it is recognized that expenses occurred.

The most traditional and widely used gift is that of tobacco. Usually in the classic twist form and often wrapped in a yellow, white or red cloth[1], tobacco has a long history in aboriginal traditions as either a public gift of respect and thanks and as a private offering to the land and spirits one wishes to pay tribute to. Other traditional gifts are cedar, sage and sweet grass in some groups. I have found that gourmet coffee is acceptable in modern times as can be any quality fruit in season, fish or game.

In Short: The giving and receiving of gifts in the Native world have a long and traditional history. However, neither the giving nor the receiving of a gift carries with it any sense of debt or owing. Gifts are symbols of relationship and valuing.

Applications: While the giving of gifts is highly approved of, it is not recommended to publicly gift one person above others. A gift that benefits the group, or various personal gifts for each is more appropriate. Remember the penchant for not standing separate from the group.

Gifts, as inducements, should be viewed with this in mind. While it may work, it traditionally has no value and induces no debt in the receiver.

The receipt of a gift is an excellent opportunity to practice the appropriate response in the language of the giver.

See also: <u>Cultural and Intellectual Property</u>, <u>Spirituality</u>, <u>Patronage</u>

LANGUAGE & SPEECH

"La lang"

A different language is a different vision of life. -Federico Fellini

Language is the soul of a culture. Languages are not like codes where you can match one collection of letters with another collection and come out with the same meanings. Beyond words, languages have a syntax, an order in which one puts those words, which in turn reflect different *paradigms* of thought and process. Phraseology carries with it nuance and emotion and meaning beyond the bare translation of the words themselves. Within language are pitch, rate and tonality, which can expand or contract the very meaning of the words themselves.

Language also carries with it identity and, with that identity, a belief in a common understanding of both culture and history. Most multi-lingual folks will quickly let you know that many things do not translate with exactness and some things do not translate well, if at all.

A case in point came a year after a potlatch where I was invited to speak at the funeral service. Potlatches can be very expensive events and the second potlatch was partially an additional memorial service and partially to include the people who couldn't make it to the first service. A family member said to me, "You are coming to the potlatch" with a slightly higher pitch at the end of the sentence. In my cultural sense of politeness, I said that I wasn't coming. In my mind, this was taken as a question and I was helping a poor family save expense of feeding and gifting me twice.

In reality, I later found out, it was a reminder of duty/respect and a statement of fact, given in a way that was open ended in order to not require that I answer. It took a while to get back in the good graces of this family.

Cultural languages in North America have had a troubled past. During the periods of forced residential schooling, which lasted in some places until the early 1980's, children were severely punished and shamed for using their native language[1]. Many languages have died out over the last 100 years. Consequently, there are often generational gaps with only a few Elders and cultural scholars actually speaking the language regularly. Realizing the disaster of the loss of language, many tribes and bands have set about a strong revival of language instruction.

The fluency in traditional language or in revival of languages varies widely among First Nations and tribal groups – from traditional being primary to English (or French in parts of Canada) being primary. The residue of this language destruction has many consequences ranging from Elders who refuse to speak anything other than their original language (especially to outsiders), to shame from those who don't know the language, and to pride in its resurgence. The crossover result to the visitor is often a collage of Native only speakers, mixed language speakers, English only speakers and a *pidgin* called 'village English' that mixes the syntax, rhythm and *patois* of multiple languages. This idiom of 'village English' is, in itself, a cultural identity trait – separating those who understand it from those who don't and thereby defining the group.

When the visitor becomes confused by an odd phrase, confusing inflection, or mixed syntax, it is necessary to understand that the experience of language, for some of these folks find English as a second, third or even fourth language. At the same time, language and culture reflect each other even when the language is no longer spoken commonly. Language and values and culture are threads in the same cloth. Each reflects the other and each affects the other even in its absence.

When speaking to a group, the presentation itself is given relatively high value in addition to the content. There should be an economy of speech, the impression of calm control and the impression that the thoughts given have been well thought out in advance[2::44]. Formal presentations are considered important and are rarely 'off the cuff'. It is a verbal skill seldom accomplished by the young.

Gesturing during formal presentations (pointing, moving arms, tapping the table) is observed considerably less often than with Western speakers, with Native speakers using slower movements and for the most part, ones closer to the body[2:49] with less expansiveness and more subtlety. One is expected to be paying attention to the thoughts expressed rather than the diversions created by movement.

If there is more than one speaker, the Western expectation is that there will be a relationship in topic or some form of acknowledged transition. This is not an expectation in the Native world – each speaker chooses his own topic and there are no required transitionals[6:59] nor do questions require answers.

Similarly, when the audience responds with statements or questions, it may be on any subject spoken of during the meeting or something completely new.

Remember, the culture and history of most Aboriginal groups is orally transmitted. This oral tradition has been recognized by the United States, Canada, Australia, the United Nations and many other governments as accurate, historical record on which to base legal decisions. The tradition of remembering with accuracy, what was said or done, is built into the very fabric of life. Consequently, be careful of what you say – it will be remembered and there will be trust in that memory.

In Short: Native languages are often the carrier and the adhesive of the culture but they are in disarray. There is considerable resentment and a profound sense of loss
T

that is seen in the community over this issue and no doubt as to where to focus this frustration. This loss is seen as a constant reminder of forced assimilation into Western culture.

Applications: Listen for meaning and emotion rather than strict word usage.

Learn a few words/phrases, especially ones of understanding or appreciation. Learn to pronounce them well and find out whether there are differences in pronunciation or meaning, even among closely related groups. There is nothing like knowing and using some of the local language to develop solidarity and to express respect. There is also nothing like using it poorly to show a lack of preparation and a sloppiness in thought processes.

The syntax of statements and questions may be inexact. It is pitch and tone that help differentiate the two, but this rule (see above) is not absolute.

Absolutely avoid idioms, historical references and abbreviations. Remember, their history is different from yours. As insightful as the pronouncements of Thomas Jefferson or Alan Greenspan may be to you, those references can draw a confusing blank to people who don't have a reference point to them. Phrases like 'over my head', 'a cold day in hell', 'out of sight-out of mind' or 'carpe diem' may seem to add panache to your presentation but may, in fact, distract from any understanding.

Similarly, avoid long presentations and verbosity. Keep your presentation succinct and in language that is understandable across a wide range of education and experience.

See also: Nonverbal, Silence

NON-INTERFERENCE

"Mahsh Ikt"

I have never been able to conceive how any rational being could propose happiness to himself from the exercise of power over others -- THOMAS JEFFERSON

Rugged individualism was a phrase used by Herbert Hoover in 1928 to describe mythical Americans taming a country. That phrase has come to constitute a picture of values embedded in western, <u>capitalistic</u> society. These values include competitiveness, influencing, argument, and pressure as a mode to success, to power and to control. It is a picture built on implied unevenness, on the win/lose dichotomy, and on a sense of superiority, which then requires inferiority in order to function.

With that picture in mind, Aboriginal cultures, with their ideas of consensus, appear tightly controlled and restricted. Nothing could be farther from the truth.

Consensus in the world of First Nations is not about requiring everybody to fit into a mold but rather an attempt to respect all opinions and to not anger or disturb any individual. Most of these groups have an ethic that each person is unique and in their uniqueness was given a view and knowledge of the universe that is every bit as 'correct' as any other.

Dr. Clare Brant, a Mohawk and a psychiatrist notes that, "This principle essentially means that an Indian will never interfere in any way with the rights, privileges and activities of another person"[1]. Dr. Brant goes on to say interference, which includes questioning in the life, beliefs or opinions of another is forbidden, regardless of the consequences to that person unless such interference is specifically requested. Even commenting on the behavior of another is considered rude.

The life of the traditional hunter-gatherer requires considerable individual decision-making. The historical consequences of decisions concerning life/death, edible/poisonous, eat/starve, and locate/lost in the North Country can be severe. Mutual respect for another person's knowledge mattered less as to why they made that decision than that they made it successfully. A cultural understanding that the Creator is intimately involved with each person's understanding and knowledge makes second-guessing another a type of sacrilege.

Additionally, active questioning of another's decision can easily be seen as adversarial and combative – traits not conducive to small community coherence. Criticism is unacceptable.

In Short: Indigenous philosophies lean heavily toward individualism, despite the apparent contradiction of the needs and desire for consensus. A person's understandings and behavior are his/hers alone. Except where behaviors endanger the community, they will be tolerated.

Applications:

In negotiations and planning, try not to see dissent as a blockage to be overcome but rather as an opportunity to address problems before they become expensive down the road.

Your 'private' life, memos and overheard discussions will not be immune from the community picture and knowledge of you and your values. How you behave must be coherent.

The politics and policies of power are likely to have adverse consequences in developing a working relationship – or any relationship at all.

Folks will not try to 'change your mind' as much as give you their reasoning as to why they might pursue a particular course of action.

See also: The Personal Connection, Family, Consensus, Spirituality, Power

HUMOR

"Mamook Hee Hee"

Natives who beat drums to drive off evil spirits are objects of scorn to smart Americans who blow horns to break up traffic jams. -Mary Ellen Kelly

Of the Indigenous cultures I have had the pleasure of participating in, and in contrast to the picture of the stoic and stern Native, humor was a large part of social and familial interactions. The format and styles change from group to group but wordplay, teasing, self-deprecating or heartfelt belly laughter are a common occurrence[2]. Humor is never used at the expense of others. It is an act of mutuality intended to enjoin people, to bring them together.[3]

However, humor doesn't translate well. What is funny in one culture or language may not be funny in another and the potential for misunderstanding and offence is high. In particular, the western traits of sarcasm, irony, puns, hyperbole and understatement, as well as tone of voice can be unusually counterproductive to the user's intent[1]. This doesn't mean that the same artifacts don't exist in Native culture, just in different ways and under different rules.

A review of many aboriginal stories will find a character (Coyote and Raven are common) who are know as tricksters – constantly playing jokes on humans and on themselves. Concurrently, many of these same humorous episodes are also lessons in humility and ego.

All humor is essentially an 'inside joke'. The commonality of experience and language is what creates the common understanding necessary for a joke to work. Due to the fear of offense (or ridicule), most humor is expressed within small in-groups or between good friends.

In Short: Humor is culturally specific and what is funny to you can easily be offensive to another with a different worldview. Humor is most often dependent upon the closeness of your relationship and the similarity of your value system.

Applications: Consider a short story about yourself or your company as an intro to a presentation. Include personal history, not your resume'. Such things as where your family is from and what life was like where you were growing up have more impact than your financial or academic successes in life.

Consider something other than jokes as your icebreaker at lectures and meetings.

Be especially careful in the use of sarcasm and other forms of humor in employee relations.

See Also: Family, Politeness, Silence

Ggax Dadeghae\

If there is one thing that can be identified as a major cause of confusion and the appearance of arrogance, it is the belief that there is one way to do things and one way only. Often it is so built in by our schooling and our culture and is bound to our being so tightly that it becomes almost impossible to realize that we are doing it.

Sometimes when I would ask a question, I found that the answer that was given confused me even more – not so much that it might be incorrect but it was so often outside of my tight constraints of meaning and how meaning is attributed.

Ggax Dadeghae was my first introduction into the Upper Ahtna way of naming and describing things. In western nomenclature, Ggax Dadeghae is the Marsh Hawk or Northern Harrier which would then go on to provide a latin name and then describe its coloring, wingspan, weight, habitat and so on. A useful system, no doubt, but not the only system.

When I asked Ruth H. about the meaning of the name she told me that it meant "rabbit packs it's bags and leaves". The meaning of the name was synchronous with its eating habits and its effect on the environment. The nomenclature is functional first and then finding further information would be acquired through conversation with Elders and hunters.

The characteristics of the flora and fauna that constitute the environment of the people dependent upon it is often based on eons of observation and on the information gleaned from its relationship with and place in the life of that world.

OBSERVATION

"Natish"

*You will accomplish more and travel farther safely if your primary thought is 'be aware'
rather than beware. Be Alert, not a lert.*   Lessons for my son, C. Wright

In many places throughout this book, I have mentioned the acuteness of
traditional senses. Not withstanding psychological and emotional sensitivities, I would
like to expand on the value and perceptive uses of the physical senses in the person
living a traditional, isolated or very rural lifestyle. Though many Native people now
live in mixed culture communities and in urban worlds, the early training in the rural
environments remains a major tool in their repertoire. For most of the ones over 35
years old, the following scenario was not so very long ago

A hunter-gatherer lives in a world defined by nature. This is not the camping
experience of vehicles, GPS, compasses, paper maps, emergency locator beacons,
store bought camouflage clothing, binoculars and freeze dried ice-cream. There were
no helicopter rescues, short wave radios, cell phones, space blankets, Gore-Tex
clothing, or synthetic sleeping bags.

To seriously live on the land in those places and times allowed for a minimum
of equipment and a maximum of internalized knowledge. The necessary knowledge
came from your own experience and that shared by those around you. As very young
children, Native people learn primarily by watching and listening[4:62]. Independence,
self-reliance and self-discipline are values begun in earliest childhood[4:64, 67]. In the
harsh environments of the arctic and sub arctic, the cost of failure can mean
starvation and death.

Imagine, if you will, that it is early October in the far north of Canada. You are
part of a village of some 40 or so people, mostly related, and looking forward to seven
months of serious winter. For the next six or seven months, the temperature will hover

around minus twenty degrees Fahrenheit with dips to minus sixty, the rivers and lakes will be frozen with ice several feet thick and various depths of snow will cover everything.

You are one of the few young adults in the community and it is your job to help provide food for the band. In the arctic north, there is never assurance that there is enough. In your hands lie the survival of your grandparents and your young children. Alone, you set out with your knife, bedroll of blankets, rifle, and a small supply of dried food seeking a moose or other large game animal that will feed many people.

A moose can travel more than one hundred twenty miles (196km) in a season(1)(2)(3) and can weigh seventeen hundred pounds(1)(2)(3). You are walking on uneven ground and are not the only flesh-eating predator on the taiga.

How clear must your memory be regarding directions and landmarks, especially in an area you may never have been in before? What must be your level of knowledge to know and predict the weather and to judge the rivers? How detailed must your understanding of habits and habitats be – not only of your quarry but also of those that might consider you food or a threat? Even if fortune is with you, how do you transport several hundred pounds of meat many miles to home. How do you feed yourself and maintain your health during this journey.

If you are unsuccessful, your family and friends may starve. If you misjudge the weather or the trail, you may not live to return.

You have about 3 weeks to accomplish this. Good luck!

In Short: The point of this is not to glorify a tough lifestyle that many of our ancestors also lived. The point is that for many of the folks that I know in the North Country, it is their own lives I am describing.

The ability to observe accurately and analyze that observation is more than a mere skill, but a cultural heritage and a constantly reinforced inherent attribute(4:62)(5:8).

Applications: The only application that I wish to present here is the simple emphasis on other chapters relative to your own presentation, in appearance and in character. Observations of your presentation and behavior will be shared quickly.

See also: Smell, Silence, Dress

Patronage
"Mamook Ko'pa Papa"

Patronage, the giving of jobs, positions and contracts to favored people has a long and honorable history in the Native world. Survival in harsh environments and a complex interrelationship of family/clan/tribe require that you substantiate your position by giving to the group(s) which have helped you to survive. Even the value of sharing has a hierarchy.

In the U.S., federally recognized native tribes have a variation of sovereign nation status. State and Federal laws regarding patronage and _nepotism_ have questionable application and/or rare enforcement. There are a variety of federal 'specialty' laws allowing for variations on civil rights for minority populations, such as native preference authority in bidding, workforce hiring, and taxes.

In addition to the general reasons set in the first paragraph, many tribes are small in population. There is often a limited work force and one person may wear many organizational hats.

Another aspect of reasoning for this is that Native people are relatively new to the western work-world and are often in need of appropriate forms of training and experience. As the cultures and values are so different, and the formal educational background may have gaps and limitations, the necessary experience may take a while.

Finally, going back to the first paragraph, 'jobs' (that is duties for pay, especially grant required or funded) may not be given to a person because they are the best qualified or the most liked. In fact, they may be neither qualified nor liked. There is the question of balance, of respect or duty due to other families, clans or other various relationships. Each leader or Council is constantly aware of the desire to maintain harmony in tribal relationships first and foremost. Relatively temporary or minor 'jobs', whether well performed or not, should not be confused with anything important.

In short: Expect negotiations and contracts to strongly focus around choice of vendors, bidding requirements and hire/fire authority. Understand that at least one benefit of any project has to be the enhancement of life within the tribe. That translates often to employment and the support of families.

Applications: Preplan your timelines for the unavoidable fact that some portion of your work will have to be considered training.

Instruct your on-site representative(s) of this situation and to not make an issue of it themselves but to report any resulting problems to the head office and legal departments. There is no sense in the creation of widespread discomfort with or avoidance of your site representatives.

Prepare your contracts with qualifications regarding limitations on pricing variations considerably outside of market standards.

Maintain a single, consistent representative who has good relations within the organization in order to minimize difficulties with touchy areas.

See also: Family, Power, High Context, Who & Why

POLITENESS
"Mamook Kloshe"

Acts are never merely acts. They are also signals of attitude. Those signals, however, are often culture specific. Rupert Ross, <u>Dancing with a Ghost: Exploring Indian Reality</u>

As you enter the indigenous world, many of the things you learned at your Mother's knee no longer apply. Facing and interacting with a Native audience, whether of one or many, often has a startling effect on westerners. The faces in front of you look to be of stone, emitting little information in either expression or other non-verbal mode. The social lubricant of western manners – the smile of greeting, the signals to talk or to not talk, the please and thank you's, the silence combine to give the naïve Westerner the impression of anger and resistance, of sullenness and distrust[2].

Actually, nothing could be farther from the truth. If that were the true feeling in the group, you would never have been invited to the meeting in the first place (or else nobody would have shown up). What you are experiencing is the native form of respect and openness to what you have to say. A lack of prejudgment is inherent in many traditional cultures as each person may have personal knowledge and insight that is peculiar to his or her experience.

Another politeness, in the native way, consists of considerable personal conversation prior to any form of business. Business, in the Western tradition, is not a high priority as compared to family, friends, weather, hunting, or children. The Native way is highly concentrated on relationships and connections between people – to rush primarily into business is poor form and indicates an attitude of uncaring concerning the person and what is truly important.

The handshake is another area where form and function differ. The firm, strong, aggressive grip that is the mainstay of Western business is not in style among indigenous people. In the Aboriginal world, handshakes are a sign of friendship and greeting – the acknowledgment of an interpersonal relationship in respect. It is given without pressure or strong grip, which is considered a mark of power relationships.

My experience with Native peoples is that they are not much interested in small talk or common Western verbal politeness phrases. If, while visiting a family, food is served, it has always been my understanding that your participation was an implicit offer. Once you have been told that you are 'Welcome, any time', that is exactly what is meant – ongoing specific invitations are unlikely(5:67).

The use of singular and plurals can confuse the Westerner. The Koyukon Na-Dene will use the third person singular (he/she) when talking to a single person and the third person plural (they) when talking to two or more. This is another aspect of politeness and the avoiding of confrontation by indirectness(5).

Avoidance of issues, especially ones concerning spiritual power, luck, medicine power, sexuality and anything else that is considered too personal or, in some cases, too dangerous, is not unusual(5).

Personal space varies among Native people both by custom and by position. The average space between Western people is usually over 18 inches. With the Inuit and most Indians, less than 18 inches is normal(7:60).

It is not unusual, though a bit perplexing, to find that the person you are talking to is standing at a ninety degree angle position to you(7:62). It is likely that this position reduces visual interference and is performed in a manner that suggests intense listening.

In Short: Take the time to know the values and interests of the community or individual you are addressing. Greet people with friendship and camaraderie first – establish the relationship, then business can be dealt with in the proper atmosphere.

Applications: In a broad spectrum of indigenous cultures, expressions of individual praise and gratitude are embarrassing and impolite, especially in front of others. In the native world of equality, singling one person out, whether for praise or condemnation, and in the presence of other members of the community violates the social rules and gives the appearance of one person standing above or below others[1:3].

In many groups, strong eye contact or staring intently at someone is considered rude and a power play. It sends a signal that you consider that person in some fashion inferior[1:3].

Even hello's and goodbye's are often unnecessary with many indigenous people[3:22][4:1]. One can see that someone else is present. That something is finished is sufficient reason to leave, parting words are not needed to complete what is obvious.

Avoid the extra firm handshake, instead replying with equal pressure and strength.

If you ask a question and get no response, or a totally unrelated response, think again about your question. Was it intrusive or too personal?

See Also: Language, Appendix A – the difference between Indians and whites, Family.

MISC. NON-VERBAL

"Kumtucks Ko'pa Weght Natish Kwolan Kun'amokst Tumtum"

What you do speaks so loud that I cannot hear what you say. -Ralph Waldo Emerson

Native people are very adept at reading each other's non-verbal messages that stay largely invisible to non-natives. As with all non-verbal understanding, familiarity is the key and the high contextuality of most native societies makes non-verbal information quite commonly understood correctly among members.

A Native friend once told me, "You white people smile, a lot! Makes us nervous". In the non-verbal literature, there are two clearly different types of smiles: The duchenne, or real smile that reflects actual joy and fake smiles. Fake smiles cannot invoke certain involuntary muscles of the forty-four muscles in the face. They are a little less symmetrical and stay on the face longer than natural smiles.[1] This is not the place to go into the neurological substrate of smiles but let it suffice to say that the two types of smiles are quite noticeable to the experienced observer. Rural Native people are some of the best visual observers on the planet – their lives and survival often depend on it.

While non-verbal messages occur in every culture, there can be considerable differences in meaning between cultures. Western speakers expect listeners to display cues that indicate they are paying attention – such things as smiling, leaning toward the speaker, good eye contact[4]. Native audiences gaze around, letting the words and associated meanings not be distracted by visuals and usually presenting a relaxed posture and minimal expression in order to avoid influencing the presenter rudely. It is silence, itself, which signifies that attention is being paid.

Handshaking was covered previously but to review: Handshakes are meant to offer respect and friendship. They are consequently gentle and relatively quick. This is usually not the place for the power shake.

In some groups, such as the Yupik Eskimo, raising the eyebrows indicates agreement[2] where in other groups it can constitute surprise or even doubt.

Posture should reflect a cooperative, thoughtful stance, not the assertive, aggressive posture of combat. Along with posture should come position. Native people are sensitive to power plays and indications of inequality. Unless it is the standard of the group, do not stand to speak at a meeting but rather, copy the patterns set by others. Standing taller than the others, looming over them, looking down are all signals of disrespect.

Prolonged and direct eye contact is often considered rude and impolite – it can be seen as defiance, superiority or a lack of trust[5:7]. Often people, even friends, will talk while looking off in the same direction. Eye contact should be fleeting and erratic – especially with Elders.

However, by never looking at the face, you would miss many clues. In general, Westerners either look directly into the eyes or tend to make judgments based on lower face cues such as compressed lips, smiles, or tightness. My experience with Native people shows that the upper part of the face carries more information – though subtle and fleeting. It has been in paying attention to the direction of the speaker's gaze, the movements of small muscles around the eyes and the widening of the eyes themselves that the information is provided[6:47, 51, 55, 56]. The meaning of each of these is contextual, and the skill in assigning meaning will improve with familiarity.

Personal space is reserved for established personal relationships. This is not the backslapping, shoulder patting, arm punching crowd. It is also a group with strong moral feelings against displays of intimacy such as public hugging and kissing.

Yet, in family traditional culture, touch is used frequently as an essential expression of friendship[5 p.8]. The dominant western culture of the U.S. only accepts physical closeness in intimate relationships but in many Native cultures, proximity provides display and perception of truth and honesty[5:9].

Vocalics, or the rate, pitch, tone and timbre of the voice are strong conveyers of emotion and meaning. Loud voices are out of place – the image given is a lack of control and consequently a lack of true power.

In listening to Elders speak on formal occasions, I have noticed a fairly consistent repetition of important points a minimum of three times – usually spoken with a different pitch and clearer. This is somewhat akin to your old teacher tapping the chalk on the blackboard, which served as a hint that this is something you should remember for the test.

Now for a little verbal/non-verbal: Uh-huh, um-m-m, O.K., sure and head nodding. Certainly, these are vocal intonations but often with meanings other than what is indicated. As indicated elsewhere in this book, most aboriginal people think that Westerners talk too much. Add to that, the understanding that they have been subject to the power of western domination for many years and western teachers, priests, bureaucrats seem to require a response, certain vocal and gestural artifacts have come to take place(5:16). Often this head-nodding, mumbled appearance of agreement is closer to a patronizing artifact intended to give you the impression that you are being heard and not necessarily that there is agreement on content or plan.

While these responses appear to indicate agreement, you might be unhappily surprised when the purported agreements don't come to fruition. To understand this, you must look carefully at your own presentation. A barrage of information, orders, directions can be seen as superiority in action and a simple passive resistance is to simply agree on the most minimalist terms. Most Native peoples prefer to avoid confrontation and, if it makes you go away just by shaking their head, great.

In Short: Forget you ever heard the joke: "If you can't dazzle them with your brilliance, then baffle them with your ……" Ha! People whose historic and cultural skill is reading the natural world and who are comfortable with silence will sense immediately the inconsistencies of BS. They are not likely to confront you but simply leave you with your inadequacies.

Applications: Probably the most important thing to stress here is to know that you don't know what you think you know. Non-verbal can mean different things in different cultures. Both giving it and the lack of giving it have ramifications.

Neither group has grown up with the understandings associated with the non-verbal actions of the other group. There are simply no appropriate assumptions that you can make about meaning without the time for observation and familiarity necessary to get a feel for the mannerisms and the flow of the group you will be negotiating with.

See also: High Context, Non-interference, Observation

Tsin'aen, ugheli kulaen

Earlier in the book, there was a short discussion about learning as much of the local language as is possible and about learning politeness, humility and appreciation first. Native people have been discounted for so long and their cultures dismissed so completely that it often becomes a very pleasant surprise to find that a visitor or a guest has taken the time and put in the effort to show respect by honoring the host.

Simply saying thank you, or its equivalent, is a good start. In the western world, we often use it perfunctorily, without much thought, as a social lubricant. In the high context world, however, it is not always a good thing to make one person stand out from the crowd, to single somebody from the group. Instead, it is better manners to recognize somebody as part of the group, a reflection of group values.

Tsin'aen is a word that is the equivalent of 'thank you' but the addition of *ugheli kulaen,* which literally only means 'it is good, nice', comes out to mean, "Things are good now that you are here" in local understanding. The importance of this little addition shows a level of interpersonal cooperation and interdependence and acknowledging the appreciation of working together.

POWER & RESPECT

"Skookum-Mitlite Kloshe Tumtum Kopa"

The leader innovates; the manager administrates. The leader focuses on people; the manager focuses on systems and structure. The leader inspires; the manager controls. The leader is his own person; the manager is a good soldier. The leader sees the long-term; the manager sees the short-term. The leader asks "what and why?"; the manager asks "how and when?" The leader does the right thing; the manager does things right. - Warren Bennis

It's not the easiest matter to translate the concept of power across the cultural divide. Power, as in affecting the process and the outcome of a project or interchange is considerably different in the majority of the Native bands with which I am familiar. Power, in the Western way is most often associated with control – the ability to require that things be done, how they are done and when they will be completed. Control is most often achieved as an absolute and the hierarchy is pyramidal with gradations from the top down.

In the Native world, power is more closely related to influence and influence is dependent upon the perceptions and desires of others. This is not to say that there are not very strong political leaders but their position is also dependent upon the support of equally strong cultural leaders, spiritual leaders and the ever-acknowledged Elders. These leaders also depend upon the views, desires and beliefs of those for whom they speak.

The leader in the Native community rarely, if ever, makes unilateral decisions that affect the community. The community, you will know by now, is all of its members, values, spiritual aspects, land, tradition and sub-groups. Human influencers will be composed of groups of men, women, clans, Elders, youth and political organizations along with mixed combinations of these groupings within the sphere. The merits of the discussion will not be limited to physical results like profit and loss or even jobs and housing. The characteristics that affect the final decision will include aspects of tradition, values, history as well as spirituality, trust level and need.

Some organizations are based on a more Western model than others are and specific personnel can make decisions internally. However, the role of the community should always be considered carefully, as it is basic to the way of thinking in the worldview of Native peoples.

Power in the Native sense requires being respected by the vast majority of the constituents. Respect is, in turn, based on traditional values and a history of giving for the betterment of the community and being involved in, and respectful of, community members and activities.

In Short: Power or authority is seldom absolute in the Native community – especially involving business. If business appears to affect the community, the community will make their feelings known. The in-group and the out-groups will be clearly defined by the community and, in the end, it is important to stand with those who voluntarily 'allow' you to lead. Leadership is not based on control as much as it is based on influence.

Applications: Make yourself or your representatives known in the community as well as in the perceived halls of power.

Preplan your project, as much as possible, so that the community clearly benefits, in their terms of benefit.

Listen to community concerns as valid despite their unclear connections within your values system.

See also: Family, Who & Why, Cultural and Intellectual Property, Patronage, Politeness, Elders

SILENCE & PATIENCE

"Halo Noise -.Klat'awa Klahwa"

"It is better either to be silent or to say things of more value than silence. Sooner throw a pearl at hazard than an idle or useless word; and do not say a little in many words but a great deal in few." - Pythagoras

Early on in my Alaskan career, I was making connections with various people in the widely dispersed communities. The Pastor of a local church branch, which primarily served a very rural Native community, was also fairly new and seemed like an all around good sort for the Alaskan bush except for his consuming love of all things Native. He had the Native culture idealized rather than as a functional reality.

Anyway, Bill desperately wanted to learn more about 'being Native' and asked an Elder who lived across the road to teach him. The Elder didn't respond for several times but eventually gave in and told Bill to show up the next morning at 9AM to be taught.

Promptly at 9AM, Bill knocked on the cabin door, was let in and given a cup of coffee. He sat, all abuzz, waiting for the Aboriginal wisdom to fill him. The Elder told him to sit and learn and then said nothing more. Soon it was 10AM, then 11 and Noon – still the Elder said nothing. Bill was sweating profusely and thoroughly confused.

Finally, at 2 in the afternoon, the Elder stood up and announced, "Next lesson tomorrow" and went out to water his sled dogs[4].

Perhaps the first and most noticeable faux pas the person unfamiliar with aboriginal ways will find is that he/she finds themselves constantly interrupting. Silence is much more common in the Native worlds than it is in the majority of Western societies. This reveals itself not only in the overall bulk of conversation but also in the spaces between words, sentences, thoughts and responses. In Western conversation, silence lasting more than two seconds indicates the end of the present portion of a conversation similar to a period at the end of a written sentence. By three seconds, others are expected to begin talking[1:350]. In Communications lingo, this is referred to as a 'turn exchange'. In the Indigenous world, pauses are consistently longer[2:4] I have found that pauses even between words may be ten or more seconds and the end of a turn at conversation or subject may require thirty seconds or more, depending on the individual speaker and situation.

Another use of silence that is confusing to Westerners has to do with getting to know one another. It is normal for Westerners to talk and to ask questions in order to get to know another person. In the Native way, it is appropriate to observe others and to show them the respect of non-interference prior to deciding whether or not to know them[3:21].

At the same time, both cultures may use extended silences to close topics that participants are no longer interested in pursuing. These conflicts help emphasize the need to develop familiarity with any particular group before risking your business plan on your presentation.

As with many characteristics in the aboriginal world, patience has roots in concepts of time and eons of experience. Life is understood to be cyclical and things happen when the time is right. Seasons, rainfall, the arrival or departure of game, the abundance of forage – all are inexact to our time but in tune with their own times.

Patience is a virtue learned at an early age. Children learn to sit quietly at long ceremonies by age two[3:19][2:13]. This quietness training is not merely for the purposes of not distracting or disturbing adults. It is part of a much wider life training for observing and learning, having a base in survival modes of the forest, tundra or sea. Experience has shown that most things arrive when they are ready but how would one know when that might be other than being observant of the signs. Non-interference dictates that one being is not in control of another but of oneself, paving the way for participating with the other as an equal being.

For Western thinkers, this concept in the business world is quite difficult to comprehend. In the native world, timelines, reports, even meetings are not considered imperative nor unequivocal but rather that if they are missed, they will either present themselves again or the time was not right

In Short: Aboriginal people often have a considerably different use of pauses and silence than is considered usual in the Western world. Depending on the context, silence can mean different things.

Native peoples are often not tied to the same sense of responsibility to time and deadlines as is usual in the Western business environment.

Applications: The more you fill in what appear to be empty spaces, the more confusing and complex the discussions will become.

A Western way of speeding up conversations is to provide what appears to be the missing word or concept. This annoying habit is impolite in western society and much more impolite in Native society.

Timelines should have a built-in variance. Tie fiscal responsibilities to defined administrative and/or physical accomplishments. If, for example, you need a report by a certain date, it is useful to attach further funding to the acceptable receipt of that report, and to send a reminding email a week previous to the reports due date.

Be careful to differentiate between the Native concept of patience and the Western concept of passive resistance. Patience allows for further movement whereas passive resistance connotes an adversarial stand.

See also: High Context Society, Time, Politeness, Appendix A # 1, Language

SPIRITUALITY

"Saghalie Tyee Tumtum"

The most beautiful thing we can experience is the mysterious. It is the source of all true art and all science. He to whom this emotion is a stranger, who can no longer pause to wonder and stand rapt in awe, is as good as dead: his eyes are closed. - Albert Einstein

The word here is spirituality, not religion. Native spirituality is inexorably intertwined with every aspect of the universe they inhabit. Early explorers and missionaries found complex and inclusive cosmologies of which the spiritual realm was integral. There were also religions among the tribes – various *avatars* and visions that developed large and small followings.

Christian churches of the day were equally integrated into the structure of many of the governments and lives of those same early explorers. Recruitment and *proselytization* are an integral part of most Christian sects and were used by many colonizing cultures as an additional arm of conquest that didn't require government funding.

Aboriginal spirituality, in congruence with other standards of individuality is quite inclusive of variances. Many Indigenous people felt comfortable accommodating Christian teachings with their own existing modes of belief. After all, they too had a supreme entity, plus saint, angels and devils are not so far removed from spirits and shamans. Epic battles, heroic figures, dastardly enemies and extreme weather activities were included in many a winter tale in their lodges long before the appearance of the new culture. That there were unseen forces that affected the lives of men was consistent with their own belief systems.

Others became Christian simply in order to not be economically or physically punished for not doing so. The onslaught of conquering and dominating societies, with both secular and religious arms, waged war against Native spirituality. An extremely large portion of the enforced and vicious schooling was less about education than it was about submission and assimilation. Children were taken from their parents and punished severely for any indication by dress, word, action or appearance that was indicative of their originating culture.

Today, there are many Native people strongly involved with the Christian theology. Native spirituality, however, remains integral within the ever-present teachings of the culture itself. For Aboriginal spirituality involves considerably more than attending church. Aboriginal spirituality involves every aspect and action of daily life. The concepts of respect, tolerance, individuality, good and bad fortune, consequences and actions are tightly intertwined with the need for balance and proper relationship.

In a cosmology where all things may have relationship to all other things, the concept of respect must accompany every interaction of consequence.

In Short: There is a specific Native spirituality, which is quite compatible with many western religions. However, it may not be readily apparent as it is melded into many aspects of life: Values, morality, hunting, gathering or ecological success, illness and recovery, good and ill fortune for a small sample. It is spirituality without dogma and reflected within the individual.

Applications: Religion remains an inappropriate discussion point in a business relationship.

Due to the severity and contemporary nature of the larger societies reactions to the practice of Native spirituality, it remains a touchy point among many cultures.

Spirituality is relatively unexplainable. Each persons understanding of it is individual and personal.

See also: Individuality, Cultural and Intellectual Property

Smell
"Humm"

Smell is a potent wizard that transports us across thousands of miles and all the years we have lived"
                                                                    - Helen Keller

Other than assuring ourselves that we do not offend and that, if possible, actually present as pleasing, we seldom give more than passing interest to the odors our bodies present.

By doing this, we defeat ourselves more often than we know. The sense of smell is one of the most evolutionarily ancient and longest lasting senses that we possess. The olfactory nerves in the nose are, of all the body's nerves, those wired most directly to the brain with the fewest intermediate relay points[1]. In matter of fact, there is only a single relay point between smell cells and the *hypothalamus*, gateway to the *limbic system* which controls much of social, sexual, memory and maternal behaviors[2:4][3][5]. It is so direct that it initially bypasses the *cerebral cortex*[3] and reactions related to smell are markedly less considered cognitively but rather are immediate responses based on memory and emotion[4:150]. Another way of saying this is that people physically react to smells that they do not even realize they are smelling[4:149] and this reaction can bring up memories that calm, stimulate, relax, evoke, frighten, increase alertness (or vigilance), or arouse[9][10].

"One thing we do know for sure is that North Americans are arguably the most uptight culture on earth about smell. To them, no body odor is a good body odor," says a leading scientific book on the effects of non-verbal behavior[11]. This is not so with other cultures for who smell is one of the many carriers of social and survival information

It is not simply that a person's hygiene is in question, but emotional state, illness, personal associations[4:150][12], stress level and perceptions of intent can be conveyed merely by scent.

In Short:

The major point here is that you are already an outsider, different, foreign. Every point by which you advertise that difference will accumulate and will be a point of reference, a topic, by somebody. It is not a bad thing to be different - native cultures are dynamic, creative and interested in possibilities. However, the more emphasis you put on those differences, the more the distance will be perceived between your culture and theirs by the listener. The larger the perceived difference, the more invidious become the questions of trust and values.

Societies with a long hunter/gatherer tradition actively use the sense of smell in sophisticated ways seldom considered by those inundated by the commercial/industrial smells of modern society. Smell can tell of weather change, food palatability, presence of game, fertility of soil, potability of water, direction to take the hunt and many more highly sophisticated and necessary pieces of information.

While the thought of a protocol on smell might seem a bit far-fetched, the reader might be interested in a recent military document titled, *Establishment of Odor Response Profiles: Ethnic, Racial and Cultural Influences* being reviewed by the National Academy of Sciences and provided by the Pentagon Non-Lethal Weapons Program[13].

Meanwhile, simply ask any former cigarette smoker if their sense of smell changed after they quit. They can certainly smell when someone near them has had a cigarette!

Applications:

People in relatively rural settings or in essentially isolated social groups are likely to have a more extensive and sensitive sense of smell than those living mainly in industrial or heavily populated areas. A change in scent will be noticeable. The potential reaction to that change is not to be taken for granted.

Between cultures, differing scents often result in different meanings. While the human nose can distinguish between up to 10,000 different odors[2], there are few odors that have universal meaning. Those of you involved in marketing may be interested in knowing that one of the few scents which is universally considered pleasant, is Cola[7] [8].

The best bet for a visitor is the limitation of artificial smells as much as possible. Items such as deodorant, aftershave, scented shampoos/soaps/body washes, and colognes should be reduced to the absolute minimum of non-existence. What is eaten or smoked before an important meeting, as well as where you were eating and smoking, and even with whom [4b] can distinguish you as 'similar or different'.

Environmental fragrancing is not simply a new age development but is a world-wide facet of both science and business[6] [8]. Don't let garlic breath or cigars sour a sweet deal. Simple cleanliness will serve you well with indigenous people and, in rural, water-poor areas, even that can be suspect.

See also: Observation, Non-verbal

TIME

"la-a-a-a-a-ly ahnkuttie"

"Modern man thinks he loses something; time; when he does not do things quickly. Yet he does not know what to do with the time he gains; except to kill it." - Erich Fromm

"Cultures dance to different drummers. Chronemics [*the study of time*]is probably the most discussed and best-researched nonverbal code in the intercultural literature"(1).

One of the hardest, most confusing areas for westerners to understand, especially western business people, is that there are multiple views of time itself. Few will deny that time is an important part of the communicative environment. The study of human aspects of time is called Chronemics and perhaps the most confusing and trying cultural gulf consists of the ways of using and seeing time - known as monochromic and polychromic.

There were originally two Greek gods of time – Kronos and Kairos(5)(9:296). Kronos (Chronos, Kronus) was the god of the clock – segmented, sequential, ordered, directional and somehow limited. Kairos was the god of time and opportunity, conceptually noting circularity and rhythms. Kairos was used to refer to the concept of personal time, that which was important to a given individual, the "right" time, "best" time or "most appropriate" time.(3) Kairos posits truth as relative to circumstance(4).

A monochromic (Chronos) time view stresses the linearity of time and sees its use as a sequence of discrete events and as directional. Time is often viewed as something tangible that can be wasted, spent, made or saved(1). This form of time is a controlling influence that western business people know too well. We are inundated with appointments, clocks and schedules, with day-planners, timecards and digital beepers. All of us grew up with mental reminders or cultural _memes_: *Time is money; A day late and a dollar short; Time and tide wait for no man; Quality time; Just in time; Time marches on.* In monochromic time, events are scheduled one item at a time and this schedule takes precedence over interpersonal relationships [6].

Time also has a directional orientation. Cultures and individuals may place emphasis on or reference to the past, present or future. At least in the hunter-gatherer based cultures that I am most familiar with, folks are present oriented and past referenced. This means that the situation at hand has the highest priority but reflections on what is done now will relate to cultural and historical guidelines.

This orientation is so strong that some groups have few words for the future and consider it 'engee' or forbidden to talk of the future[7:20]. Saying what will be done, accomplished or take place is akin to fortune telling and is disrespectful to the powers beyond themselves and such an insult is likely to bring bad fortune in reprisal for such impudence. The word 'time' in translation from many Native languages is a verb, not a noun[8].

As common a part of our lives as time attention has become, it wasn't always so. Only with the industrial revolution of some 150 years ago, did this obsession with time really get going. Previous to that, most of us were farmers or hunters ourselves, with a much larger and considerably more vague sense of time. It took us a century and a half and Henry Ford and Charles Taylor to get to our present obsession but for many native people, this sense of segmented time is less than 50 years old and often only peripherally part of their own world.

Polychromic (Kairos) views of time have little regard for artificial schedules and stress informality, people-centeredness, multiple simultaneous activities and the importance of context[1][6]. Most native peoples see time as relative to the rhythms of nature, the focus at hand, the opportunity of the moment. This form of time is freeing and without constraint.

Time can become a force of applied or resistant pressure. Time even relates to psychological impressions of respect and regard or views of intelligence – your views of time are a reflection of your cultural values.

In Short: The concepts and use of Time are not the same for all people or all places. Not only do most indigenous people have a different sense of time in the circular vs. linear sense, but they also may have very different ideas as to what is considered a priority than western business people. Issues dealing with family, food provision, potlatch, funerals and other cultural occasions that historically related to physical survival will often take considerable precedence over matters of 'mere' business.

Application: Be very careful here – the use of and reaction to time is potent. Indigenous approaches to time vary widely from most western perspectives and misunderstandings are the, unfortunately, normal result.

Appointments are variable and can be blocked or interrupted by many things that make little sense to the western businessperson. Few meetings begin on time. Consensus is a necessity for many local decisions and it is considered rude to have some people hear all the information and others hear less. Consequently, rather than they waiting for you, which is also rude, you are expected to be able to wait for their comfort level and appearance.

Other common points of conflict come into play with time-required signatures, scheduled reports, workday scheduling, deliveries, trip planning. Give yourself plenty of time for delays and preparations. Always remember that 'business' is likely to not be the highest priority. Families and entire villages will take days and weeks off for funerals, grieving, hunting and regional gatherings – these understandings need to be a factor in your scheduling.

See also: Non-verbal, Silence, Consensus

ELDERS

"Elip"

"Old age ain't no place for sissies." - Bette Davis

Elders are the backbone of most Native communities. They are the history and the language; they are the survivors and the wisdom. With the elders stand the continuity of the culture – past, present and future.

However, it is not like the Association for the Advancement of Retired People (AARP), which sends Americans offers of membership at age 50. Elders can't be recognized by presentation of a membership card or signet ring. There is no designated period of longevity required. One can be elderly and treated with respect but not be considered an Elder. Even a considerably younger person may be considered an Elder if the community recognizes him/her as such. In fact, many people in the community may disagree on whom they consider an Elder.

In reality, only other Elders decide who is involved in their discussions. As a rule, Elder status is seen as such due to respect for their knowledge and perspective. Historically they have a lifelong familiarity with the language although this may be changing as the present generations pass on. They are most often a living example for the rest of the community of life based on cultural values as recognized by that community. Although they are likely to be the grandparents of one family, their sharing of knowledge and beliefs is normally quite apolitical.

Elders are *de facto* survivors of the cultural, economic and physical wars of their comparatively long lifetimes. The wisdom and knowledge that they share is not only ancient but is often functionally adapted by their long experience.

In the various cultures and subcultures in which I have lived, other characteristics come into play. For instance, family and clan status are influential in

Spokes to the Wheel

the identification of an Elder as are previous positions held or services provided. The orientation of the present political powers also effects community standing and reception.

The Community may or may not respect or support an Elder at any given time and dependent upon circumstance. One of the characteristics of an Elder, which I have observed, is the overcoming of some life difficulty that is recognized by the group (e.g., alcoholism, deaths, illness) and the strength to take unpopular stands. It is an apparent conflict that the indigenous groups with which I have been involved include a great social pressure to avoid public conflict and to achieve unanimity in decisions, yet the elder who stands against the tide is often the saving grace from destruction by inaction and is highly respected.

Elders often teach by the traditional method of example and, in speaking, are more likely to use stories and metaphor. A direct answer would violate the inherent right of others to see the meaning by themselves.

In Short: In contrast to much of modern western society, Elders are venerated and appreciated in the world of Indigenous peoples. They are the gatekeepers of the culture and are integral both to its past and to its future.

Application: Elders should be respected and appreciated as wondrous resources of knowledge and understanding. They are not tools for alignment or pressure.

If an opportunity comes to address an Elders group, do not expect an answer or a decision. It will not be made without further discussion and only 'when the time is right'.

- 106 -

Every issue of importance will pass by the Elders in some fashion. Consider what you know of their perspective in every action and proposal if you hope to succeed.

See also: <u>Appendix A, #5</u>, <u>Language</u>, <u>Family</u>, <u>Power</u>

EPILOGUE

"Opoots Tumtum"

Now you have some understanding of the old ways, the traditional ways, the convention around interaction in many First Nations communities. These quiet, unwritten, often unspoken semi-rules of interpersonal activity affect most relationships, business or otherwise.

This is also the time to say, "It ain't necessarily so". For these are traditional folkways in traditional societies. Throughout these writings, there has been emphasis that cultures are dynamic and always in a process of change. Cultures intermix and separate; generational rule is replaced by the next generations' perspective and knowledge; focuses wax and wane in importance amidst changes in the social, physical and economic environment. The new wave of young lords moves from youth into adult power and responsibility, and the amalgamation begins once and again.

As with the concepts of individuality among Native cultures, occasionally whole generations have a different perspective and different understandings than the generations preceding them. This is not a concept that is specific to Aboriginal cultures - one aspect of youth is the extension and definition of self in most societies.

Many of the aboriginal youth that I am familiar with are full of anger and determined to change the status quo with the dominant societies around them. High unemployment rates, make-work jobs, questionable and poorly funded training opportunities and overrepresentation in the prison and justice systems combined with a long history of broken treaties, land misappropriations and uneven social justice have left a simmering, sometimes boiling distrust of dealings with westerners. (See notes)

The attributes of nations under domination and pressure come into play. Passive resistance in the face of overwhelming power is a classic reaction throughout the world and throughout history. Bursts of militancy periodically find their way into the headlines of the regional and national news.

So, here you have it – Aboriginal people are different from Western people, and Aboriginal people are quite similar to Western people. It all depends on the perspective and the expectations that you put into the lens through which you are looking.

Even traditional customs change over time and some people place more emphasis on them than do others. The basic rules of respect and tolerance apply in most situations. It is my experience, throughout the world, that the 1950's vision of motivation by psychologist Abraham Maslow, the 'hierarchy of needs', has been a useful reference point in dealing with people of all cultures and subcultures I have had contact with. In a nutshell, it prescribes that physiological and safety needs have to be satisfied before higher needs can even be dealt with. You have to meet people where they are, not where you expect or wish them to be.

The fulfillment of the requirements of each need is dependent upon the fulfillment of the needs below it. When any lower need is threatened, it immediately becomes the life priority. Protocol properly belongs with Safety needs – as the outsider, respecting the rules of the group are the only access to belonging and community.

When the lower needs have a present or recent memory of not being met – whether in the individual or the society – they maintain a high priority. Even in business dealings, not paying attention to history perils your negotiations. Ultimately, our base is that we are all human beings.

THOUGHTS

"Mamook Tumtum"

So many ways have come to mind on how to end this book. One of the joys of writing is that there is a space for personal rambling.

We are all so involved in the worlds we know, that it is difficult to really believe that other worldviews truly exist and continue to function. Most of us have enough trouble getting by with what we do know that it presents a major conundrum to seriously consider deviating from our accustomed paths in any serious fashion – it seems to threaten our survival as we know it.

This is one of the true tragedies of modern life. We are born with innate curiosity and creativity. That creativity has found quantum physics, which has verified the multiple paths that are possible to any individual – as Buddhism discovered by introspection a millennia ago – there are many spokes to the wheel.

It appears that we have made quantum leaps in science, medicine and technology. We can communicate across the planet at electronic speeds, have volumes of every conceivable kind of information at our fingertips, can destroy entire civilizations at the press of a button, and can amass untold personal wealth.

Yet, there are costs and trades for these wondrous abilities. Our 140 channel, wide screen television sets assault us daily with news of war and famine, of disease and pestilence, of dwindling resources and mental aberrations. New cures seem to be replaced with new diseases. With each apparent advance comes the threat of being overwhelmed and returned to a level of existence that we can conceive of but do not actually remember.

The psychic load that each of us carries appears enormous.

We can peer into the beginnings of the universe and into the heart of an atom. Can we see any better into the heart and mind of the person aside of us, down the street, around the corner? Indeed, this is the problem we have faced, and not solved since the dawn of time – and the source of much of our difficulty yet today.

I cannot help but believe that, in reality, this may be the ongoing source of the vast majority of the other difficulties. We have a few things yet to learn if we, as a species, are to survive.

GLOSSARY

"Kumtuks Wawa"

Aboriginal: See Native

Aristotelian logic: A form of deductive reasoning consisting of a major premise, a minor premise, and a conclusion; for example, *All humans are mortal*, the major premise, *I am a human*, the minor premise, therefore, I am mortal, the conclusion. 2.Reasoning from the general to the specific; deduction.

Athabascan: A group of related North American Indian languages including the Apachean languages and languages of Alaska, northwest Canada, and coastal Oregon and California.

Avatar: A prophet or holy person. The incarnation of a Hindu deity, especially Vishnu, in human or animal form. 2. An embodiment, as of a quality or concept; an archetype.

Capitalism: An economic system in which the means of production and distribution are privately or corporately owned and development is proportionate to the accumulation and reinvestment of profits gained in a free market.

Cerebral cortex: The extensive outer layer of gray matter of the cerebral hemispheres, largely responsible for higher brain functions, including sensation, voluntary muscle movement, thought, reasoning, and memory.

Clan: A traditional grouping, similar to a fraternity, of a bloodline following either from the paternal or maternal side that carries both relationships and responsibilities beyond the family line. Clans provided for social and organizational needs as well as definitions of marriage restrictions.

Collectivistic: Having the traits of a collective society. A collective society works together on an enterprise and shares the results. Of, relating to, characteristic of, or made by a number of people acting as a group: a collective decision.

Consensus: An opinion or position reached by a group as a whole. 2.General agreement or accord: government by consensus.

Cosmology: 1.The study of the physical universe considered as a totality of phenomena in time and space.   2. a. The astrophysical study of the history, structure, and constituent dynamics of the universe.   b. A specific theory or model of this structure and these dynamics.

Culture: There are many attempts to adequately define this term. Ultimately it includes the totality of information presented to, and learned by, you from your social group. It is the conglomeration of rules, values, meanings, ways of thinking, and even options available provided by your family, spiritual teachings, community and significant others from conception onward.

Dichotomy: Division into two usually contradictory parts or opinions

Faux pas: A social blunder

First Nations: See Native. Used primarily in Canada.

Gestural: A motion of the limbs or body made to express or help express thought or to emphasize speech.

Hammurabi: Babylonian king (1792-1750) who made Babylon the chief Mesopotamian kingdom and codified the laws of Mesopotamia and Sumeria.

Holistic: a. Emphasizing the importance of the whole and the interdependence of its parts.

      b.Concerned with wholes rather than analysis or separation into parts.

Hypothalamus: a portion of the brain, it activates, controls, and integrates part of the nervous system, the endocrine processes, and many bodily functions, as temperature, sleep, and appetite. Part of the reticular activating system controlling consciousness, attention, concentration.

Indigenous: See Native

Limbic system: a group of related nervous system structures within the midbrain that are associated with various emotions and feelings, as anger, fear, sexual arousal, pleasure, and sadness.

Matrilineal: Relating to, based on, or tracing ancestral descent through the maternal line.

Matriarchal: A woman who rules a family, clan, or tribe.   2. A woman who dominates a group or an activity.   3. A highly respected woman who is a mother.

Memes: A unit of cultural information, such as a cultural practice or idea, that is transmitted verbally or by repeated action from one mind to another.

Moiety: A bilateral division of clans or phatries that provided a relative balance of forces within a culture.

Native: The oldest known and continuous existing inhabitants of a region. Used interchangeably with indigenous and First Nations.

Nepotism: Favoritism shown or patronage granted to relatives, as in business.

Paleolithic: Of or relating to the cultural period of the Stone Age beginning with the earliest chipped stone tools, about 750,000 years ago, until the beginning of the Mesolithic Age, about 15,000 years ago.

Paradigm: One that serves as a pattern or model. A set of assumptions, concepts, values, and practices that constitutes a way of viewing reality for the community that shares them, especially in an intellectual discipline.

Patois: A regional dialect, especially one without a literary tradition. 2.b. Nonstandard speech. 3.The special jargon of a group; cant.

Patrilineal: Relating to, based on, or tracing ancestral descent through the paternal line.

Phatry: A grouping of Clans that traditionally worked together or had compatible roles.

Pidgin: A simplified form of speech that is usually a mixture of two or more languages, has a rudimentary grammar and vocabulary, is used for communication between groups speaking different languages, and is not spoken as a first or native language. Alsocalled contact language.

Potlatch: A ceremony involving significant family or community events common to many Athabascan Indians but occurring in other indigenous cultures under other names.

Potlatches were historically celebrated for many major events such as harvests, a good hunting season, remembrances of historical events, the ending of conflicts, and many other important events. In modern times, potlatches are primarily seen as part of funeral and grieving processes.

Propinquity: Proximity; nearness, kinship., similarity in nature.

Proselytize: To induce someone to convert to one's own religious faith. 2.To induce someone to join one's own political party or to espouse one's doctrine.

Squat: to occupy unused premises to which one has no legal right.

Traditional: The passing down of elements of a culture from generation to generation, especiallyby oral communication. 2.a .A mode of thought or behavior followed by a people continuously from generation to generation; a custom or usage. b. A set of such customs and usages viewed as a coherent body of precedents influencing the present. 3. A body of unwritten religious precepts. 4. A time-honored practice or set of such practices.

Western: pertaining mostly to the scientific view popular in North America and Europe – one of Aristotelian logic, rationality, segmentation and linear patterns as typified in the pursuit of science.

Worldview: 1.The overall perspective from which one sees and interprets the world.

2. A collection of beliefs about life and the universe held by an individual or a group.

Definitions provided by www.dictionary.com

Chinook Jargon/Interpretation

This 'trade language' – a combination of words from various Pacific Northwest tribes, French, English and Spanish – was developed by early sailors, traders and mountain men in order to converse with the local tribes. It was first known around 1785. By the early 1900's the language was out of popular use but words and names from the language have been found as far away as Interior Alaska, Alberta Canada, east to Illinois and down into California. Some words can still be heard on Seattle streets today.

As explained in the chapter on language, words may have multiple meanings depending on context, connection, sequence and who is saying it – male/female, age, social position

Preface - Elip Chee Mamook = <u>Before original work</u>

Chee, *adv., adj.* = New, fresh, original, just now, recent

Elip , *adv.* = First, before, beginning, prior, ahead, senior, elder, former, original

Mamook, n., v = Labor, work, exertion, deed, to accomplish, task

Introduction -Chee Klatawa = <u>Start new</u>

Chee, *adv., adj.* = New, fresh, original, just now, recent

Klatawa, *v* = to go, travel, attend, flow, migrate, start, tread, leave, begone, get out, depart

Rule #1 - Mamook Kloshe Ikt = <u>First auspicious work or labor</u>

Ikt or Icht, *adj.* = One, once, a unit (also a or an)

Kloshe or Klosh, *adv., adj.* = good, well, well enough, affable, amiable, apt, auspicious, beautiful, beloved

Mamook, *n., v* = Labor, work, exertion, action, deed, accomplish, to do, task

Chapter 1: Who and Why – Klatsta, Kahta – <u>Who? Why?</u>

Kah-ta, adv. = Interrogative, Why?

Klak'-sta, pron. = Interrogative, Who?

Chapter 2: Protocol – Ikt Kloshe Ooahut Wawa – <u>One Good Way to Talk</u>

Ikt, adj. = A, An, One,

Kloshe or Klosh, *adv., adj.* = good, well, well enough, affable, amiable, apt, auspicious, beautiful, beloved

Ooakut or Ooahut, n. = a road, a path, the way

Wawa, v = to talk, spak

Chapter 3: What is Culture? – Iktah Tumtum Tillikum? – <u>What is the Spirit of a People?</u>

Iktah, pron. – Interrogative. What?

Tillikum, n. = People, relations, relatives, associate, family, folks, friends, kin, kindred, band, tribe, fellow nation

Tumtum, n., v. = The heart, the will, opinion, intellect, intention, estimate, memory, mind, soul, spirit, thought

Chapter 4: <u>Contact</u> - .Elip Chako Kunamokst = <u>Original coming together</u>

Chako or chah'-ko or Chahco, *v.* = To come, to approach, to be or become

Elip, *adv.* = First, before, beginning, prior, ahead, senior, elder, former, original

Kunamoks or Kunamoxt, *adj, prep.* = Both, together, amidst, among, beside

Chapter 5: <u>High Context Society</u> - Kloshe Kopa Konaway Kumtucks = <u>To know all around about well</u>

Kloshe or Klosh, *adv., adj.* = good, well, well enough, affable, amiable, apt, auspicious, beautiful, beloved

Konaway, *adj.* = All, every, total, universal, aggregate, entire, the sum, the whole

Kopa, *adv., prep, conj.* = At, according to, around about, concerning, to, into, with, towards, of, there, in that place, than, for, from, on, during, through, instead of

Kumtucks or Kumtux, *v., n.* = To know, understand, be acquainted with, learn perceive, ascertain, recognize, imagine, believe, to be wise, knowing, knowledge, wisdom, sense

Chapter 6: <u>The Personal Connection</u> – Skookum Sikhs - <u>Solid Friend</u>

Sikhs or Shikhs or Six, *n.* = Friend, companion

Skookum, *n., adj.* = Strong, a ghost, able, solid, potent,

powerful, vehement, tight, tough

Chapter 7: <u>History, Whose?</u>- Hyas Ahnkuttie Yiem = <u>Very ancient story</u>

Ahnkuttie, *adv.* = Formerly, before now, long ago, anciently, age

Hyas, *adj., adv.* = Large, great, very, the general term

for size, wide, big, vast

Yiem, *v., n.* = A story, tale, anecdote, to relate, to tell a story

Chapter 8: <u>Consensus</u> - Tumtum = <u>Opinion together</u>

Kunamoks or Kunamoxt, *adj, prep.* = Both, together, amidst, among, beside

Tumtum, *n., v.* = The heart, the will, opinion, intellect, intention, estimate, memory, mind, soul, spirit, thought

Chapter 9: <u>Cultural & Intellectual Property</u> – Nika Tillikum, Nika Tumtum, Nika La Lang – <u>My Kin, My Knowledge, My Language</u>

La lang, *n.* = The tongue, a language, dialect, tribe

Nika, *pron.* = I, my, mine, me

Tillikum, *n.* = People, relations, relatives, associate, family, folks, friends, kin, kindred, band, tribe, fellow nation

Tumtum, *n., v.* = The heart, the will, opinion, intellect, intention, estimate, memory, mind, soul, spirit, thought, knowledge

Chapter 10: <u>Dress</u> – Iktas = Clothing

Chapter 11: <u>Education</u> - Mamook Kumtuks = <u>To work on knowing</u>

Kumtucks or Kumtux, *v., n.* = To know, understand, be acquainted with, learn perceive, ascertain, recognize, imagine, believe, to be wise, knowing, knowledge, wisdom, sense

Mamook, *n., v* = Labor, work, exertion, action, deed accomplish, to do, task

Chapter 12: <u>Family</u> –Nika Tillikum = <u>My family</u>

Nika, *pron.* = I, my, mine, me

Tillikum, *n.* = People, relations, relatives, associate, family, folks, friends, kin, kindred, band, tribe, fellow nation, population, person

Papa, n. = a Father

Chapter 13: Clans, Moieties & Phatries - Sit'kum La lang – Parts of the Tribe

Kokshut, v = split, tear, torn, cleave, hurt, shatter

Sit'kum, n., adj. = a part, fraction, middle, some, a piece

Tsugh, n., v. = to split, to become split

La lang, n. = The tongue, a language, dialect, tribe

Chapter 14: Gifting - Potlatch = a present or free gift, expecting no return

Cultus or Kultus, adj. = unmeaning, useless, paltry careless, futile, immaterial

Potlatch or Pahtlatsch, n., v. = a gift, to give, a lot, cede, expend

Chapter 15: Language – La lang = Language

La lang, n. = The tongue, a language, dialect, tribe

Chapter 16: Non-Interference - Mahsh Ikt- To leave alone

Ikt or Icht, adj., = alone, once

Mahsh, v., adj = to leave

Chapter 17: Humor - Mamook Hee Hee – To Make Laugh

Mamook, v., adv., = to make; to do; to work

Hee Hee, n., = laughter, amusement

Chapter 18: Observation – Natish Nan-itsch - See

Natish, v. = to see, look; look for; seek; observe; view

Chapter 19: Patronage - Mamook Ko'pa Papa – to work for a Father

Ko'pa, adv., prep., conj. = for; at; around; about; concerning; instead of

Mamook, v., adv., = to make; to do; to work; act; action

Chapter 20: Politeness - Mamook Kloshe – affable, do nice

Mamook, v., adv., = to make; to do; to work; act; action

Kloshe or Klosh, adv., adj. = good, well, well enough, affable, amiable, apt, auspicious, beautiful, beloved

Chapter 21: Non-Verbal – Kumtucks Ko'pa Weght Natish Kwolan Kun'amokst Tumtum - Know by listening and seeing from the heart.

Ko'pa, adv., prep., conj. = for; at; around; about; concerning; instead of

Kun'amokst, adj, prep = both alike, together

Kwolan or Kwolah'lie, n. = the ear; to hear

Kumtucks or Kumtux, v., n. = To know, understand, be acquainted with, learn perceive, ascertain, recognize, imagine, believe, to be wise, knowing, knowledge, wisdom, sense

Natish or nanitsch, v. = to see, look; look for; seek; observe; view

Tumtum, n., v. = The heart, the will, opinion, intellect, intention, estimate, memory, mind, soul, spirit, thought

Weght = Also, more, again

Chapter 22: Power & Respect - Skookum-Mitlite Kloshe Tumtum Kopa – Strong and a place of goodness from the heart

Kloshe or Klosh, adv., adj. = good, well, well enough, affable, amiable, apt, auspicious, beautiful, beloved

Ko'pa, adv., prep., conj. = for; at; around; about; concerning; instead of

Mitlite, v., = to sit down, stay at, reside, remain, have, inhabit, abide, dwell exist, dwell, be present, linger/possess

Skookum, n., adj. = Strong, able, solid, potent,

powerful, vehement, tight, tough – also ghost or demon

Chapter 23: <u>Silence and Patience</u> - Halo Noise - .Klat'awa Klahwa – <u>Devoid of noise – Move slowly</u>

   Halo, adj. =Not, none, absent, no, all gone, devoid, vacant, without

   Klahwa, adv. = slow, slowly

   Klat'awa, v. = Go, move, attend, flow, leave, start, tread, travel

   Noise = noise, noisy

Chapter 24: <u>Spirituality</u> - Saghalie Tyee Tumtum – <u>Uppermost chief, known in the heart</u>

   Saghalie, n., adj. = Up, above, high, upper, uppermost, over, heaven, sky

   Tyee, n., adj. = A chief, superior, boss, king, the Deity

   Tumtum, n., v. = The heart, the will, opinion, intellect, intention, estimate, memory, mind, soul, spirit, thought

Chapter 25: <u>Smell</u> – <u>Humm</u>

   Humm, n. = Odor, nose

Chapter 26: <u>Time</u>

   la-a-a-a-a-ly ahnkuttie = Time immemorial. There are literally dozens of words for time – both specific and general but none for the concept of time.

Chapter 27: <u>Elders</u> – Elip – <u>Elders</u>

   Elip, adv. = First, before, the superlative, beginning, prior, ahead, senior, elder, former, original

<u>Epilogue</u> - Opoots Tumtum – <u>End Thoughts</u>

   Opoots, n. = The fundament, the posterior, the tail, anus, end, rectum, stern, back, backside

   Tumtum, n., v. = The heart, the will, opinion, intellect, intention, estimate, memory, mind, soul,

spirit, thought

<u>Thoughts</u> - Mamook Tumtum – <u>to Use the Mind</u>

   Mamook, v., adv., = to make; to do; to work; act; action

   Tumtum, n., v. = The heart, the will, opinion, intellect, intention, estimate, memory, mind, soul, spirit, thought

<u>Glossary</u> - Kumtuks Wa wa – <u>Know the Words</u>

   Kumtucks or Kumtux, v., n. = To know, understand, be acquainted with, learn perceive, ascertain, recognize; imagine, believe, to be wise, knowing, knowledge, wisdom, sense

<u>Acknowledgements</u> – Mahsie Okoke Kumtucks – <u>Thanking those of knowledge</u>

   Okoke, pron. = This, that, it, these, those

   Mahsie, v. = Thank, Thanks, to give thanks, to praise

   Kumtucks or Kumtux, v., n. = To know, understand, be acquainted with, learn perceive, ascertain, recognize; knowledge

Translations and Interpretations adapted from:

<u>The Chinook Jargon and How to Use It: A complete and Exhaustive Lexicon of the Oldest Trade language of the American Continent</u> (1909), Rainier Printing Company, Inc, Seattle,

<u>Dictionary of Chinook Jargon</u>, Frederick J. Long, Compiler, (1909), Lowman & Hanford Co, Seattle, WA WA – reprint by Coyote Press, Salinas, CA

Dictionary of the Chinook Jargon: The Indian
Trade Language of the Pacific Coast (1906),
T.N. Hibben & Col, Victoria, B.C. Canada–
reprint by Coyote Press, Salinas, CA

ACKNOWLEDGEMENTS

I came up to the north country of rural Alaska somewhat prepared, or so I thought. After all, I had lived and worked with a myriad of cultures and subcultures that were estranged and outside of the mainstream of the western world for most of my life. My youth had been spent in neighborhoods of first generation immigrants working in the industrial factories of southern New England. For the next 20 years, with credentials that didn't accumulate as fast as the various systems required, my mental health career was always involved with the folks that those with higher credentials didn't want to be involved with – Latinos/Latinas, Blacks, legal & illegal immigrants, alcoholics, drug abusers, gays & lesbians, abusers and the abused.

I had lived in environments that ranged from the Mayflower families of Maine, the industrial East, experienced life on the mean urban Eastern streets and the barrios of Los Angeles to the rural mountains of Northern California, Oregon, and backwoods Washington. I had worked in factories, prisons, stores, farms, detoxes, and shelters; been on welfare and food stamps, seen the inside of jails, been a single parent, a Hippie, sheet metal worker, salesman, construction worker and organic farmer; lived as a homeless person, on a production line, in the cash economy, in the world of barter and trade, as a skilled tradesman and as a professional.

And, in the vernacular of many Alaskan friends, "I didn't know nuthin' yet!"

The information presented in this book is 90% experiential, bolstered by the words of academic research and literature. I freely admit I wouldn't have persevered through half of it without the sage advice, lifelong experience, practical wisdom and genuine friendship of many people. One commonality between the rural folks of Alaska and those of Maine, of Scandanavia and South America is that they will willingly share and assist – as long as you show integrity and aren't whining about your lot.

For these people, I have a heartfelt gratitude and loving appreciation:

Bruce Heaton – my first 'hiree' and first Native friend in Alaska and the one who reminded me to "shut my mouth, listen, and speak sparingly in simple language". **Ruth Hicks** of Mentasta Village and **Maggie Joe** of Chistochina Village made me dance at potlatch, let me sit at Elders meetings and gently helped me to understand their people. **Lena Charlie** of Chistochina told me of the old ways, of plant medicines and of her growing up in a village and life that no longer exist. **Glenda Ewan** of Gulkana Village quietly guided me through the intricacies of village life. **Markle Pete** of Tazlina Village who's booming laughter and serious thoughts renewed and directed me again and again. **Joe Goodlataw** of Tazlina Village who was born in and lived the old traditions, who told me stories about that existence that few yet living will ever hear. Also to **Johnny Goodlataw**, his son, current Council President, and Johnny's wife, **Irene Goodlataw** for welcoming me into their family life as a friend and quietly telling me stories of the old ways out at their fish camp. Whenever I became confused, which was often in the early years, **Lucy Brenwick,** Elder of Copper Center Village was my guide and mentor.

I need to especially thank the entire **Tazlina Village Council(s)** and all members of the **Tribe of Tazlina** for their tolerance with my moving too fast in trying to get them what I thought they wanted. We clashed more than a few times but I learned a great deal in my years with them – certainly a lot about consensus and about listening to the people. In that vein, I need to particularly focus on Council President **Gloria Stickwan** for her quiet but persistent direction; to long time Council Member **Mae Marshall** for her perpetual interest and insight in preserving both the past and insuring the future, and to her husband, **Robert Marshall** who started the modern village and who always guided as a senior Elder behind the scenes. I learned something of value from everybody.

Dr.'s **Ray Barnhardt** and **Oscar Kawagley** of the University of Alaska, Fairbanks deserve much praise for putting up with my frustrated tirades about non-functional academic bureaucracy and for guiding me through a late life graduate degree with humor and wisdom. They seemed to have survived the ordeal of advanced education and remained human. Remarkable!

There are plenty of non-native folks to thank also. **Al Slemsek** who found heaven in Alaska in 1940 and almost never left; **Floyd & Janet Wharton** who always shared coffee, meals, chocolate and stories/theories/experiences of their own Alaskan journey through many a night and who helped me persevere through tough times in my trailer on their property on the Klutina River. There is **Michael Moody** of the end of the road community of Chitina – for rafting the Yukon on a piece of foam, caring for his fellow man, living a subsistence lifestyle and for keeping his dreadlocks and gentle attitude. **John Gilbert**, also of Chitina, is thanked for his music, his experience and his knowledge of many Alaskan aspects. **Crystal Best**, my first friend in Alaska, for her indomitable courage, strength and humor (and rare a capella gifts) while surviving five (?) husbands, two stalwart children, a lifetime inside a native corporation and every needy straggler who she came across.

A special gratefulness goes to **Linda Moreau**, Chair of the Teacher Assistant Program at Red Deer College in Alberta and friend who introduced me to the many faces of Canada, provided me with sustenance and supported my research in innumerable ways. Without her support and encouragement, this tome might never have been completed.

Another thank you goes again to **Linda Moreau** and **Susan LaFontaine** for emotional support, proofreading and editing. Out of the almost 30 people who said they would help, only these two actually did. Thank you from the bottom of my heart.

The list can go on and on, white, non-white and native of many tribes. Those who are not mentioned on this page continue to influence my mind and my heart.
Tsin' aen,

Dedication

To my dear Mother who passed from this earth March of 2000 at 87. Mom was born in a 1630's farmhouse in rural Maine to a Mayflower family. She was the first to leave the farm in 300 years and, with my Father, braved the industrial, immigrant world of WW II Connecticut in search of a better life.

Mom had never seen a person of color nor heard an accent. Yet her faith in the value and innate worth of all humans fostered in me an ability to go anywhere and know that I was among family. Thanks, Mom.

APPENDIX A

Included in this section are lists and sayings collected from office and village hall walls over the years. The author and origin is often unknown and is accredited where possible. However, you never know how different people are going to find the best understanding for themselves.

I don't vouch for the accuracy of these statements nor to which groups they might apply. Somebody thought these lists spoke for him or her and I present them as found.

1. Why the confusion?

What's confusing to English speakers about Athabascans	What's confusing to Athabascans about English speakers
The Presentation of Self	
They do not speak	They talk too much
They keep silent	They always talk first
They avoid situations of talking	They talk to strangers or people they don't know
They only want to talk to close acquaintances	They think they can predict the future
They play down their own abilities	They brag about themselves
They act as if they expect things to be given to them	They don't help people even when they can
They deny planning	They always talk about what's going to happen later
The Distribution of Talk	
They avoid direct questions	They ask too many questions
They never start a conversation	They always interrupt
They talk off the topic	They only talk about what they are interested in
They never say anything about themselves	They don't give others a chance to talk
They are slow to take a turn in talking	They just go on and on when they talk
The Contents of Talk	
They are too indirect, too inexplicit	They aren't careful when they talk about people or things
They just don't make sense	They just don't make sense
They just leave without saying anything	They have to say 'goodbye' even when they can see you are leaving

Found in "Interethnic Communication", Scollon & Scollon, 1981, p. 17

2. Different strokes

Native Values	Non-Native Values
Leaders are the servants	Leaders are the masters
Cooperation	Competition
Group Emphasis	Individual Emphasis
Passive	Assertive
Informal Courtesy	Formal Courtesy
Patient	Impatient
Sharing	Saving
Time is Constant	Time is Fleeting
Respect for Age	Respect for youth
Harmony with Nature	Conquest over nature
Non-verbal	Verbal
Extended Family	Nuclear Family
Tradition	Novelty
Little eye to eye contact	Direct eye to eye contact
Holistic Problem solving	Analytic problem solving
Happiness = Spiritual Harmony	Happiness = Wealth Accumulation

Spokes to the Wheel

3. Cultural Values

	Indigenous Values	Dominant Society Values
Family	Clan/muit – a quasi system of fraternalism; and prestige a dependency on individual responsibility the nearest to the clan; a greater pressure exists in the nuclear clan than anything comparable in the dominant society; a relationship gives security and identity	Nuclear family – security and prestige found within the confines of the nearest relatives and especially in the nuclear family.
Cultural Transmission	By word of mouth – oral tradition	By writing books – external tradition
Peace	Harmony – Cosmic harmony is sought; individual is concerned personally with the entire cosmos.	Personal peace – a personal harmony is sought within the individual person
Health	The body and soul are one; health is synonymous with the harmony of body and soul with nature	A scientific viewpoint is taken to the restoration of bodily health
Time	Natural time regulates their activities with a NOW orientation	Clock time regulates with a FUTURE orientation
Will Power	Fatalism; man cannot alter events and he must constantly attempt to restore all things to their original harmony	Self-determination – The world can be altered by man's will. He tries to create God
Ownership	Clan system dictates ownership – passed by tradition	Legal ownership – passed by law
Property	Communal – Using only what is needed and sharing with others	Private property – Surplus is accumulated; goods belong to one person
Security	Security is found within the family and clan = WHO AM I?	Security is found in success – WHAT HAVE I DONE?
Age	Respect for the wisdom and experience of age	Respect for the energy and vitality of youth
Structure of Society	Non- competitive; non-comparative	Competitive, accumulative
Taboos	Explain evil by spirit	Explain evil by science
Work	Work when necessary	Work for itself
Adaptability	Reason why is sought; the practicality is examined. Value is sought in the NOW	Progress is the goal
Religion	Myth and example by synthesis	Dogma and instruction by analysis

4. East/West

An Eastern Worldview: American Indian/Alaskan Native	A Western Worldview: European Immigrants/Settlers in U.S.
Group Emphasis	Individual Emphasis
Present and Past Orientation	Future Orientation
Time: Always With Us	Time- Use Every Minute
Age	Youth
Cooperation	Competition
Harmony with Nature	Conquest Over Nature
Giving-Sharing	Taking-Saving
Pragmatic	Theoretical
Mystical	Skeptical
Patience	Aggressive
Listening Skills learned first	Verbal Skills learned first
Religion: A Way of Life	Religion: Segment of Life
Should appear modest	Should put one's best foot forward
Oral	Written
Use of land	Ownership of land
As a part of Nature, they cannot own any other part of it, though sole rights of use	As the most important things on earth for whom all Nature was made, it is theirs to do with as they see they may have fit

Adapted from Drug Abuse Prevention is Everybody's Business, Pub. by MCRC, l977, pg. 9. Accessed: (Mar 20, 2002) HTTP://WWW.ANKN.UAF.EDU/ANE/

5. Dealing with Elders - 1

Initial and subsequent contact should be subtle. Visit with them, allowing time for the conversation to wander.
Allow for extended pauses, giving them time to think and decide.
If their hearing is poor, sit on the side of their better ear and make sure our lips can be seen.
Direct eye contact should be limited.
Standing or sitting at an angle can increase an elder's comfort level.
Keep you questions basic and simple
Begin the request by telling a little about yourself and how the elder could help.
Hint strongly that you would like to have their help and ask if he/she knows of someone who might be willing to participate.
Custom teaches that it is rude to give someone a firm no to a request for help, so you need to recognize that a noncommittal response might mean "no", or it might mean that the request is being considered.
If at some point the elder changes the subject more than once while you are explaining your request, you should be aware that he/she might be trying to say 'no'.
Don't force a response: if it is clearly not a 'yes', let it go, or suggest they contact you after they've thought about it.
It is important to ask before a meeting for permission to make audio or video recordings
Provide them with optional dates and the logistics.

Elders in the Classroom, Roby Littlefield 747-6866, published in "Sharing our Pathways", Vol. 4, Issue 2, Mar/Apr. 1999, page 6 http://www.ankn.uaf.edu/SOP/SOPv4i2.pdf

6. Dealing with Elders - 2

Do not ask for yourself - ask for others
Present yourself in different ways - let the elders know you (other meetings/events)
Don't Push
Go to their home - informal, Tea, walk together
Conversational not strongly structured or directive
Elders wish to see results in kids using the knowledge
Real teaching needs interaction
Learn to remember yourself - just like they did - don't just write/record

*Notes from the video "Passing On" by Mike Martz ©AKRSI 2000
http://www.ankn.uaf.edu/videos/passingonsharp.html

7. Classroom vs. Experiential Learning Formats

Experiential	Standard
Multi – sensory	Limited forms of input
Practical application	Only potential practical application
Contextual (applied in a context)	Conceptual
Active	Passive
Transformative	Mimetic
Concrete	Abstract
Oral	Notational Sophistication
Enmeshed with Community Life	Disassociation from Community Life
Functional Utility is important	Practical utility is unimportant
Intrinsic motivations	Extrinsic motivations
Global or synthesis	Compartmentalized
Flexible methodologies	Restricted methodologies
Coherent peer group	Disparate Peer Group
Subjective & Individualized	Objective & Standardized

Non School	School
The 'final authority' or expert is immediate, familiar & usually related	The 'final authority' is always distant – aide to teacher to superintendent to author
Learning is primarily active and immediately functional	Learning is primarily passive and the functionality is distant
Much of this learning is voluntary	School is a legal requirement and imposed
Learning is practical, often related directly to survival	Learning is conceptual and unrelated to the day to day activities in the community
Success is determined by individual performance in day to day life and physical survival	Success is a rating system that is impersonal, not individualized and conceptual for a potential future use.
Teachers are part of daily life and part of the community	Teachers are exclusive to the school setting
Priorities are internal to the group	Priorities are external from the community
There are no time limitations except those posed by nature and life	Exceptionally time limited and compartmentalized
Much of the learning is tactile and sensory	Minimized tactile – most learning is conceptual
Student can succeed without knowing why conceptually	Requires conceptual understanding for success
Teaching styles allow for much variation	Teaching styles are constrained by rules and regulation

8. Dichotomies

Christopher's Dichotomies	
Tribal	Westerner

Demur on Accomplishments	Maximize Accomplishments
Time orientation: Present	Time orientation: Future
Parsimonious with words	Expansive with words
Learn by observation	Learn by doing
Show skills when mastered	Show skills while learning
Situation has priority	Time has priority
Relationship important	Accomplishment important
Permissive child rearing	Directive child rearing
Early maturity	Late maturity
Eye contact is intrusive/defiant	Eye contact is required for honesty
Speak soft and slow	Speak fast & loud
Long pauses in speech	Very short pauses in speech
Group orientation	Individual orientation
Venerate age & wisdom	Forced retirement & wrinkle cream
Honor in giving	Honor in getting
Share	Save
Talk after knowing	Talk to know
Cooperation	Competition
Process focus	Content focus
Individualism supported	Individualism restrained
Conserve	Consume
Family is perpetual	Family constantly recreated
Extended family	Nuclear family
Internal	External
Holistic	Segmented
Indirect or oblique	Direct or aggressive
Give face	Save face
Synchronous	Linear

9. Guidelines for Respecting Cultural Knowledge

Guidelines for Native Elders

As one of the primary sources of traditional cultural knowledge, Native Elders bear the responsibility to share and pass on that knowledge in ways that are compatible with traditional teachings and practices.

Native Elders may increase their cultural responsiveness through the following actions:

   a. Participate in local and regional Elders Councils as a way to help formulate, document and pass on traditional cultural
      knowledge for future generations.
   b. Help make explicit and incorporate locally appropriate cultural values in all aspects of life in the community, while recognizing the diversity of opinion that may exist.
   c. Make a point to utilize traditional ways of knowing, teaching, listening and learning in passing on cultural knowledge to others in the community.
   d. Seek out information on ways to protect intellectual property rights and retain copyright authority over all local knowledge that is being shared with others for documentation purposes.
   e. Carefully review contracts and release forms to determine who controls the distribution of any publications and associated royalties.
   f. Review all transcripts of cultural information that has been written down to insure accuracy.
   g. Follow appropriate traditional protocols as much as possible in the interpretation and utilization of cultural knowledge.
   h. Assist willing members of the community to acquire the knowledge and skills needed to assume the role of Elder for future generations.

Guidelines for Authors and Illustrators

Authors and illustrators should take all steps necessary to insure that any representation of cultural content is accurate, contextually appropriate and explicitly acknowledged.

Authors and illustrators may increase their cultural responsiveness through the following actions:

a. Make it a practice to insure that all cultural content has been acquired under informed consent and has been reviewed for accuracy and appropriateness by knowledgeable local people representative of the culture in question.

b. Arrange for copyright authority and royalties to be retained or shared by the person or community from which the cultural information originated, and follow local protocols for its approval and distribution.

c. Insure controlled access for sensitive cultural information that has not been explicitly authorized for general distribution.

d. Be explicit in describing how all cultural knowledge and material has been acquired, authenticated and utilized, and present any significant differing points of view that may exist.

e. Make explicit the audience(s) for which a cultural document is intended, as well as the point of view of the person(s) preparing the document.

f. Make every effort to utilize traditional names for people, places, items, etc., adhering to local conventions for spelling and pronunciation.

g. Identify all primary contributors and secondary sources for a particular document, and share the authorship whenever possible.

h. Acquire extensive first-hand experience in a new cultural context before writing about it.

i. Carefully explain the intent and use when obtaining permission to take photographs or videos, and make it clear in publication whether they have been staged as a re-enactment or represent actual events.

j. When documenting oral history, recognize and consider the power of the written word and the implications of putting oral tradition with all its non-verbal connotations down on paper, always striving to convey the original meaning and context as much as possible.

Guidelines for Curriculum Developers and Administrators

Curriculum developers and administrators should provide multiple avenues for the incorporation of locally recognized expertise in all actions related to the use and interpretation of local cultural knowledge and practices.

Curriculum developers and administrators may increase their cultural responsiveness through the following actions:

A Establish an easily accessible repository of culturally appropriate resource materials and knowledgeable expertise from the community.

b. Include the voices of representatives from the local culture in the curriculum materials used in the school.

c. Utilize the natural environment of the community to move educational activities beyond the classroom as a way of fostering place-based education and deepening the learning experiences of students.

d. Support the implementation of an Elders-in-Residence program in each school and classroom.

e. Provide an in-depth cultural orientation program for all new teachers and administrators.

f. Promote the incorporation of the Alaska Standards for Culturally Responsive Schools in all aspects of the school curriculum, while demonstrating their applicability in providing multiple avenues to meet the State Content Standards.

g. Utilize Elders and Native teachers from the local community to acquire a comprehensive understanding of all aspects of the local, regional and statewide context in which the students live, particularly as it relates to the well-being and survival of the local culture.

h. Make use of locally produced resource materials (reports, videos, maps, books, tribal documents, etc.) in all subject areas and work in close collaboration with local agencies to enrich the curriculum beyond the scope of commercially produced texts.

i. Establish a review committee of locally knowledgeable people to review all textbooks and other curriculum materials for accuracy and appropriateness in relation to the local cultural context, as well as to examine the overall cultural responsiveness of the educational system.

Guidelines for Educators

Classroom teachers are responsible for drawing upon Elders and other cultural experts in the surrounding community to make sure all resource materials and learning activities are culturally accurate and appropriate

Teachers may increase their cultural responsiveness through the following actions:

a. Learn how to use local ways of knowing and teaching to link the knowledge base of the school to that of the community.
b. Make effective use of local expertise, especially Elders, as co-teachers whenever local cultural knowledge is being addressed in the curriculum.
c. Take steps to recognize and validate all aspects of the knowledge students bring with them, and assist them in their on-going quest for personal and cultural affirmation.
d. Develop the observation and listening skills necessary to acquire an in-depth understanding of the knowledge system indigenous to the local community and apply that understanding in teaching practice.
e. Carefully review all curriculum resource materials to insure cultural accuracy and appropriateness.
f. Make every effort to utilize locally relevant curriculum materials with which students can readily identify, including materials prepared by Native authors.
g. Provide sufficient flexibility in scheduling Elder participation so they are able to fully share what they know with minimal interference by the clock, and provide enough advance notice for them to make the necessary preparations.
h. Align all subject matter with the Alaska Standards for Culturally Responsive Schools and develop curriculum models that are based on the local cultural and environmental experiences of the students.
i. Recognize the importance of cultural and intellectual property rights in teaching practice and honor such rights in all aspects of the selection and utilization of curriculum resources (see attached bibliography for details).

Guidelines for Editors and Publishers

Editors and publishers should utilize culturally knowledgeable authors and establish multiple levels of review to insure that all publications are culturally accurate and appropriate.

Editors and publishers may increase their cultural responsiveness through the following actions:

a. Encourage and support Native-authors and provide appropriate biographical information and photographs of the author(s) of culturally oriented material.
b. Return a significant proportion of publication proceeds and royalties to the person or community from which it originated.
c. Submit all manuscripts with cultural content to locally knowledgeable personnel for review, making effective use of local and regional entities set up for this purpose.
d. Insure appropriate review, approval and access for all digital and Internet-based materials.
e. Resolve all disagreements on cultural content or distribution before final publication.
f. Always return to the original source for re-authorization of subsequent printings.
g. All content of textbooks for general curricular use should be examined to make sure it is widely accepted and recognized, and not just an individual author's opinion.
h. Honor all local conventions for recognizing cultural and intellectual property rights.

Guidelines for Document Reviewers

Reviewers should give informed consideration to the cultural perspectives of all groups represented in documents subjected to review.

Document reviewers may increase their cultural responsiveness through the following actions:

a. Always be as explicit as possible in identifying the background experience and personal reference points on which the interpretation of cultural meaning is based.
b. Whenever possible and appropriate, reviews of cultural materials should be provided from multiple perspectives and interpretations.
c. When critical decisions about a publication are to be made, a panel of reviewers should be established in such a way as to provide a cross-check from several cultural perspectives.
d. Publications that misrepresent or omit cultural content should be identified as such, regardless of their remaining literary merit.
e. Reviews of movies involving cultural themes should utilize the same guidelines as those outlined for published

documents.

Guidelines for Researchers

Researchers are ethically responsible for obtaining informed consent, accurately representing the cultural perspective and protecting the cultural integrity and rights of all participants in a research endeavor.

Researchers may increase their cultural responsiveness through the following actions:

a. Effectively identify and utilize the expertise in participating communities to enhance the quality of data gathering as well as the data itself, and use caution in applying external frames of reference in its analysis and interpretation.
b. Insure controlled access for sensitive cultural information that has not been explicitly authorized for general distribution, as determined by members of the local community.
c. Submit research plans as well as results for review by a locally knowledgeable group and abide by its recommendations to the maximum extent possible.
d. Provide full disclosure of funding sources, sponsors, institutional affiliations and reviewers.
e. Include explicit recognition of all research contributors in the final report.
f. Abide by the research principles and guidelines established by the Alaska Federation of Natives and other state, national and international organizations representing indigenous peoples.

Guidelines for Native Language Specialists

Native language specialists are responsible for taking all steps possible to accurately convey the meaning associated with cultural knowledge that has been shared in a traditional language.

Native language specialists may increase their cultural responsiveness through the following actions:

a. Whenever possible, utilize a panel of local experts rather than a single source to corroborate translation and interpretation of language materials, as well as to construct words for new terms.
b. Encourage the use and teaching of the local language in ways that provide appropriate context for conveying accurate meaning and interpretation, including an appreciation for the subtleties of story construction, use of metaphor and oratorical skills.
c. Provide Elders with opportunities and support to share what they know in the local language.
d. Whenever possible, utilize simultaneous translation equipment at meetings to facilitate the use of the local language.
e. Prepare curriculum resource materials that utilize the local language, so as to make it as easy as possible for teachers to draw upon the local language in their teaching.

Guidelines for Native Community Organizations

Native community organizations should establish a process for review and authorization of activities involving the gathering, documentation and use of local cultural knowledge.

Native community organizations may increase their cultural responsiveness through the following actions:

a. The Native educator associations should establish regional clearinghouses to provide an on-going process for the review and certification of cultural resource materials, including utilizing the available expertise of retired Native educators.
b. Native educators should engage in critical self-assessment and participatory research to ascertain the extent to which their teaching practices are effectively grounded in the traditional ways of transmitting the culture of the surrounding community.
c. Native communities should provide a support mechanism to assist Elders in understanding the processes of giving informed consent and filing for copyright protections, and publicize the availability of such assistance through public service announcements on the radio so all Elders are aware of their rights.
d. Each community and region should establish a process for reviewing and approving research proposals that may impact their area.
e. Each community should establish a process for determining what is considered public knowledge vs. private knowledge, as well as how and with whom such knowledge should be shared.
f. Native communities should receive copies and maintain a repository of all documents that relate to the local

area.

g. Native communities/tribes should foster the incorporation of traditional knowledge, language and protocols in all aspects of community life and organizational practices.

h. As regional Tribal Colleges are established, they should provide a support structure for the implementation of these guidelines in each of their respective regions.

Guidelines for the General Public

As the users and audience for cultural knowledge, the general public has a responsibility to exercise informed critical judgement about the cultural authenticity and appropriateness of the materials they utilize.

Members of the general public may increase their cultural responsiveness through the following actions:

a. Refrain from purchasing or using publications that do not represent traditional cultures in accurate and appropriate ways.

b. Encourage and support Native peoples' efforts to apply their own criteria to the review and approval of documents representing their cultural traditions.

c. Contribute to and participate respectfully in local cultural events to gain a better understanding of the range of cultural traditions that strive to coexist in Alaska.

d. Make room in all community events for multiple cultural traditions to be represented.

General Recommendations

The following recommendations are offered to support the effective implementation of the guidelines for documenting and representing cultural knowledge outlined above.

1. The Alaska Standards for Culturally Responsive Schools should be used as a general guide for any educational activity involving cultural documentation, representation or review.

2. A statewide "Alaska Indigenous Literary Review Board" should be established with representation from each of the regional Native educator associations to oversee the implementation of the recommendations that follow.

3. A statewide "Alaska Indigenous Knowledge Multimedia Working Group" should be established to examine the applicability of the above guidelines to the production of electronic media and the publication and utilization of cultural knowledge via the Internet.

4. Criteria for "product certification" of materials with cultural content should be established and implemented by regional Literary Review Committees formed through the regional Native educator associations. The "Raven" images from the ANKN logo could be used as a "stamp of approval" for each cultural region.

5. Each regional Literary Review Committee should develop a list of authorized reviewers for publications reflecting cultural content related to the respective region.

6. An annotated bibliography of the best materials representing local cultures should be compiled by each regional Literary Review Committee and published on the Alaska Native Knowledge Network web site for use by teachers and curriculum developers throughout the state.

7. The Alaska Indigenous Literary Review Board should establish prestigious awards to honor Native Elders, authors, illustrators and others who make a significant contribution to the documentation and representation of cultural knowledge.

8. Incentives, resources and opportunities should be provided to encourage and support Native authors, illustrators, story-tellers, etc. who can bring a strong Native voice to the documentation and representation of Native cultural knowledge and traditions.

9. The guidelines outlined above should be incorporated in university courses and made an integral part of all teacher preparation and cultural orientation programs.

10. An annotated bibliography of resource materials that address issues associated with documenting, representing and utilizing cultural knowledge should be maintained on the Alaska Native Knowledge Network web site.

Used with permission from The Alaskan Native Knowledge Network -
http://www.ankn.uaf.edu/standards/culturaldoc.html

10. Guidelines for Nurturing Culturally Healthy Youth

Guidelines for Native Elders

Respected Native Elders are the essential role models who can share the knowledge and expertise on traditional child-rearing and parenting that is needed to nurture the cultural well-being of today's youth.

Native Elders, as the tradition-bearers, can help nurture culturally healthy youth through the following actions:

a. Participate in local and regional Elders councils as a way to help formulate, document and pass on traditional child-rearing and parenting practices for future generations.

b. Establish traditional Elders councils for developing, nurturing and mentoring leadership potential.

c. Help implement and incorporate locally appropriate cultural values in all aspects of life in the community, especially those involving children and youth.

d. Provide guidance and assistance in utilizing traditional ways of knowing, teaching, listening and learning in passing on cultural knowledge to younger generations in the community.

e. Serve as a role model and mentor for young people by practicing and reinforcing traditional values and appropriate behaviors in the everyday life of the community.

f. Share stories and participate in story-telling opportunities in the community as a way to pass on the cultural values and traditions.

g. Assist new parents in learning the knowledge and skills needed to carry out their role as care-givers and the first teachers of their children.

h. Continue the use of traditional naming practices and help children and parents understand the significance of the names and kinship ties they have acquired.

i. Encourage, support and volunteer to assist in all aspects of the educational programs in the school, including both traditional and contemporary matters.

j. Help young people understand the world around them and how it has changed from the world in which previous generations were raised, including the interconnectedness of the human, natural and spiritual realms.

k. Assist members of the community to acquire the knowledge and skills needed to assume the role of Elder for future generations.

Guidelines for Parents

Parents are the first teachers of their children and provide the foundation on which the social, emotional, intellectual and spiritual well-being of future generations rests.

Parents, as the primary caregivers, can help nurture culturally healthy youth through the following actions:

a. Provide a loving, healthy and supportive environment for each child to grow and achieve their fullest potential from pre-natal through adulthood.

b. Establish parenting circles in the community that provide an opportunity for young parents to share their joys and frustrations and learn from each others experience.

c. Connect with parents/grandparents in the community who can serve as role models for providing a nurturing family and home environment.

d. Utilize the traditional disciplining roles of uncles, aunts, Elders and other authority figures in the community to help children learn what is right and wrong in a constructive way.

e. Participate as a family and encourage children to become actively involved in cultural activities and learn the traditional values of the community.

f. Set aside time each day and/or week for family-oriented activities, including extended family members whenever possible.

g. Make arrangements to accompany your child through part or all of a school day at least one per quarter to gain an understanding of what they are doing in school.

h. Use traditional naming practices and help each child understand the significance of the names they carry.

i. Volunteer to participate in activities that help make the schooling experiences of each child an extension of their home and community life (e.g., adopt-a-teacher program).

j. Practice the locally identified cultural values and rules of behavior in all family activities and encourage other members of the community to do the same.

k. Assist children in learning and using their heritage language.

l. Assist children to understand their family history and the heritage(s) that shape who they are and form their identity.

m. Make use of locally appropriate rituals and ceremonies to reinforce the critical events in children's lives.

n. Serve as a positive role model and mentor for your children by practicing and reinforcing traditional values and appropriate behaviors.

o. Participate in community-sponsored programs that enhance parenting skills.

Guidelines for Youth

Culturally healthy youth take an active interest in learning their heritage and assume responsibility for their role as contributing members of the family and community in which they live.

Youth can nurture their own cultural well-being through the following actions:

a. Learn all you can about your family, kinship relations and community history and cultural heritage.

b. Participate in subsistence activities with parents, Elders and other members of the community and learn the stories and lessons associated with those activities.

c. Become actively involved in local activities and organizations that contribute to the quality of life in your community.

d. Show respect to the Elders in your community by assisting them in any way you can.

e. Get involved in regional, state and national issues and organizations that impact your community.

f. Make healthy choices in your lifestyle that contribute to the wholeness and well-being of yourself and those around you.

g. Always be a good role model, show respect, and provide support to others.

h. Participate in apprenticeships with cultural experts in the community and acquire traditional conflict resolution skills.

i. Seek to acquire all the knowledge and skills associated with the "cultural standards for students" (published in the Alaska Standards for Culturally Responsive Schools).

j. Use critical judgment in the selection of popular media for reading, viewing and listening, and make sure it is aligned with your aspirations as an adult.

k. Associate with friends who can provide healthy role models that will make a positive contribution to your growth and development toward adulthood.

Guidelines for Communities, Tribes, Clans and Native Organizations

Communities must provide a healthy and supportive environment that reinforces the values and behaviors its members wish to instill in their future generations.

Communities can help nurture culturally healthy youth through the following actions:

a. Recognize that the children of the community are its future, and ensure that every child grows up secure on who they are and confident in their ability to make their own way in the world.

b. Strengthen the parenting roles as reflected in traditional kinship structures by adopting child-rearing as a collective responsibility, and make sure children know their kinship roles and responsibilities.

c. Sponsor regular parent/youth talking circles in the community.

d. Promote healthy community activities and supportive organizations by involving youth as board members and participants in all functions, meetings, workshops, and events related to community well-being.

e. Organize local and regional planning meetings that lead to a consensus on strategies for consistent support of young people from all the sectors of the community that impact their lives (home, school, Elders, church, community organizations, cultural events, media etc.)

f. Be a good role model for and engage youth in all aspects of community life, including involvement in youth-run organizations and councils and participation in Native corporation and tribally-sponsored activities.

g. Foster family and community-oriented activities on a regular basis by suspending bingo, TV and other forms of distraction for one night a week.

h. Recognize and support accomplishments of community members, including youth.

i. Whenever encountering young people and adults in the community, greet them and acknowledge their existence.

j. Foster traditional knowledge, values and beliefs in all aspects of community life and institutional practices.

k. Publish and distribute posters, announcements, buttons, calendars and other daily reminders of culturally appropriate rules of behavior and child-rearing practices as valued by the Elders.

l. Implement tribal courts that incorporate traditional healing, restorative justice and rehabilitation practices to deal with youth who have committed serious infractions of community rules, expectations and protocols.

m. Incorporate the cultural standards for communities and parents into daily life, as outlined in the Alaska Standards for Culturally Responsive Schools.

n. All youth-oriented programs and services should be administered by Native-controlled organizations at the most local level possible.

Guidelines for Educators

Educators are responsible for providing a supportive learning environment that reinforces the cultural well-being of the students in their care.

Educators (teachers, administrators, aides, counselors, etc.) can help nurture culturally healthy youth through the following actions::

a. Learn traditional child-rearing and parenting practices to link the knowledge base of the school to that of the community.

b. Recognize that student's developmental needs undergo substantial changes in early adolescence that can effect academic performance, so instructional strategies will need to be adapted accordingly.

c. Adopt curricular and instructional strategies that connect to the cultural and physical world in which the students are situated.

d. Make effective use of local expertise, especially Elders, as co-teachers whenever local cultural knowledge is being
   addressed in the curriculum.

e. Take steps to recognize and validate all aspects of the knowledge students bring with them and assist them in their on-going quest for personal and cultural affirmation.

f. Develop the observation and listening skills necessary to acquire an in-depth understanding of the knowledge system indigenous to the local community and apply that understanding in teaching practice.

g. Visit the student's homes and learn about the parents aspirations for their children as well as their expectations for you.

h. Carefully review all curriculum resource materials to insure cultural accuracy and appropriateness and assist students in making similar critical judgments themselves.

i. Make every effort to utilize locally relevant curriculum materials with which students can readily identify, including materials prepared by Alaska Native authors.

j. Serve as a role model for students by utilizing constructive forms of discipline over punishment, and providing positive reinforcement over negative feedback.

k. Provide sufficient flexibility in scheduling Elder participation so they are able to fully share what they know with minimal interference by the clock, and provide enough advance notice for them to make the necessary preparations.

l. Align all subject matter with the Alaska Standards for Culturally Responsive Schools and develop curriculum models that are based on the local cultural and environmental experiences of the students.

m. Recognize the importance of cultural and intellectual property rights in teaching practice and honor such rights in all aspects of the selection and utilization of curriculum resources.

n. Participate in community events and activities to acquire the insights needed to develop appropriate motivation and discipline practices in the school.

Guidelines for Schools

Schools must be fully engaged with the life of the communities they serve so as to provide consistency of expectations in all aspects of students lives.

Schools may help nurture culturally healthy youth through the following actions:

a. Establish an easily accessible repository of culturally appropriate resource materials and a reliable process for the daily involvement of knowledgeable expertise, including respected Elders, from the community.

b. Include the voices of representatives from the local culture in the curriculum materials used in the school.

c. Provide developmentally appropriate curricula that take into account the cultural variability of the social, emotional, intellectual and spiritual needs of each child and community, especially during the critical period of identity formation that takes place during the adolescent years.

   d. Utilize the natural environment of the community to move educational activities beyond the classroom as a way of fostering place-based education and deepening the learning experiences of students.

   e. Support the implementation of an Elders-in-Residence program in each school and classroom and teach respect for Elders at all times..

   f. Provide an in-depth cultural orientation program for all new teachers and administrators.

   g. Promote the incorporation of the Alaska Standards for Culturally Responsive Schools in all aspects of the school curriculum, while demonstrating their applicability in providing multiple avenues to meet the State Content Standards.

   h. Utilize Elders and Native teachers from the local community to acquire a comprehensive understanding of all aspects of the local, regional and statewide context in which the students live, particularly as it relates to the well-being and survival of the local culture.

   i. Make use of locally produced resource materials (reports, videos, maps, books, tribal documents, etc.) in all subject areas and work in close collaboration with local agencies to enrich the curriculum beyond the scope of commercially produced texts.

Guidelines for Child-care Providers

Childcare providers should draw upon Elders and other local experts to utilize traditional child-rearing and parenting practices that nurture the values and behaviors appropriate to the respective cultural community.

Childcare providers can help nurture culturally healthy youth through the following actions:

   a. Incorporate parents and other knowledgeable members of the surrounding cultural community to the maximum extent possible in all aspects of childcare and family services.

   b. Utilize traditional stories, toys, games, songs, language, foods and related activities whenever possible and appropriate to establish consistency between experiences in childcare and at home.

   c. Insure that all childcare workers are knowledgeable about and have first-hand experience in the cultural and family contexts from which the children are drawn (i.e., hire/train local childcare providers).

   d. Provide all childcare supervisors and workers with appropriate training and understanding of requirements in areas related to the Indian Child Welfare Act, special needs children, evidence of child abuse, FAS/FAE, health and safety issues, referral services, etc.

   e. Encourage sponsoring organizations to implement family-friendly employment practices that encourage maximum parental involvement in the up-bringing of their children.

   f. Invite traditional story-tellers to spend time with children while in childcare facilities, or take children to visit Elders in the community.

   g. Practice good hygiene at all times and teach the same to the children.

Guidelines for Youth Services and Juvenile Justice Agencies

Youth services and juvenile justice agencies should provide a supportive policy, program and funding environment that encourages local initiative in the application of traditional child-rearing and parenting practices.

Youth services and juvenile justice agencies can help nurture culturally healthy youth through the following actions:

   a. Emphasize cooperative approaches that nurture the intrinsic good in the youth with whom you work, and seek to
     minimize reliance on threats, punishment and extrinsic forms of motivation to achieve obedient behavior (i.e., focus on reinforcing good behavior over punishing bad).

   b. Implement practices that focus on prevention, traditional healing, restitution and rehabilitation as avenue of first resort in dealing with youth who have committed serious infractions of communal rules, expectations and protocols.

   c. Work with local communities to adopt correction policies and practices oriented toward education, prevention, remediation, restitution, rehabilitation and healing in culturally appropriate ways

   d. Utilize talking/healing/sentencing circles to foster a climate of introspection, support and remediation when seeking to achieve corrective action and rehabilitation.

   e. Whenever possible, promote participation and integration of youth into the surrounding society, rather than removal and separation for infractions or anti-social behavior.

f. Work with schools to provide a supportive, prevention-oriented social climate for all students and seek to retain students in a healthy environment as much as possible.

g. Engage youth in multi-media productions in which they are encouraged to portray their aspirations for the world around them.

Guidelines for Researchers

Researchers should work with local communities to help document traditional child-rearing and parenting practices and explore their applicability to the upbringing of today's youth.

Researchers can help nurture culturally healthy youth through the following actions:

a. Effectively identify and utilize the expertise in participating communities to enhance the quality of data gathering as well as the data itself, and use caution in applying external frames of reference in its analysis and interpretation.

b. Make sure that all research pertaining to child-rearing and parenting include consideration of cultural differences in everything from the sampling and data-gathering procedures to application of the results.

c. Insure controlled access for sensitive cultural information that has not been explicitly authorized for general distribution, as determined by members of the local community and participating families and individuals.

d. Submit research plans and research results for review by a locally knowledgeable group and abide by its recommendations to the maximum extent possible, including ample time for accurate data gathering to take place.

e. Provide full disclosure of funding sources, sponsors, institutional affiliations and reviewers, and supply adequate compensation for all participants.

f. Include explicit recognition of all research contributors in the final report and provide copies to all participating individuals, communities and organizations.

g. Abide by the Guidelines for Respecting Cultural Knowledge prepared by Native educators and the research principles established by the Alaska Federation of Natives and other state, national and international organizations representing indigenous peoples (see ANKN web site).

Guidelines for the General Public

All citizens must assume greater responsibility for nurturing the diverse traditions by which each child grows to become a culturally healthy human being.

Members of the general public can help nurture culturally healthy youth through the following actions:

a. Treat children and youth from all backgrounds with honor, dignity and respect and involve them in the activities of everyday life to the maximum extent possible — this is how they learn to become contributing adults.

b. Encourage and support Native peoples' efforts to apply their own child-rearing and parenting practices in the upbringing of their children.

c. Recognize that all forms of success in school and in life depend first and foremost on developing a strong sense of personal and cultural identity, and that the formative adolescent years are the most critical for defining who we are in relation to others.

d. Celebrate that which we all share in common as members of a national society, as well as all the differences that make each of us unique and serve as the basis for the local and personal identities which enrich our lives and communities.

e. Contribute to and participate respectfully in local cultural events to gain a better understanding of the range of cultural traditions that coexist in Alaska.

f. Provide opportunities for young parents and children to interact regularly with Elders and other experienced parents.

g. Make room in all community events for multiple cultural traditions to be represented.

h. Use popular media to promote positive role models for young people to emulate and to pass on the traditional teachings.

i. Ensure the accuracy and authenticity of all materials that enter the public domain depicting culturally-oriented situations and behaviors relating to particular groups of people.

General Recommendations

The following recommendations are offered to support the effective implementation of the guidelines for nurturing culturally healthy youth.

1. The Alaska Standards for Culturally Responsive Schools shall be used as a general guide for any educational activity involving nurturing culturally healthy youth.

2. Community and regional entities shall pursue the re-establishment of traditional disciplining, restitution and rehabilitation programs through tribal courts, sentencing circles, Elder's counseling and other forms of culturally appropriate remediation practices.

3. State and federal criminal justice systems and associated youth facilities shall work with local communities to adopt correction policies and practices oriented toward education, prevention, remediation, restitution, rehabilitation and healing in culturally appropriate ways, with incarceration and isolation the punishment of last resort, especially for misdemeanors and non-violent infractions.

4. The Department of Education and Early Development shall expand the focus of the annual Bilingual/Multicultural Education Conference to include an emphasis on traditional child-rearing and parenting (possibly alternating themes from year to year).

5. Each Regional Health Corporation shall sponsor an annual regional gathering around the themes of traditional child-rearing and parenting, including opportunities for men and women to meet independently to discuss their own concerns.

6. School shall sponsor opportunities for students to participate regularly in cultural immersion camps with parents, Elders and teachers sharing subsistence activities during each season of the year.

7. School districts shall provide an annual cultural orientation camp for teachers to acquaint them with the experiences and the lives from which their students come.

8. All regional Elders conferences shall include traditional child-rearing and parenting as a theme whereby the Elders are able to contribute to the development of contemporary child-rearing practices aimed at nurturing culturally healthy youth.

9. Parenting Circles shall be established in every community to provide an opportunity for young parents to interact regularly with one another and other knowledgeable community members around issues of child-rearing and parenting.

10. As regional Tribal Colleges are established, they shall provide a support structure for the implementation of these guidelines in each of their respective regions.

11. The guidelines outlined above shall be incorporated in university courses and made an integral part of all professional preparation and cultural orientation programs.

12. An annotated bibliography of resource materials that address issues associated with traditional child-rearing and parenting shall be maintained on the Alaska Native Knowledge Network web site (www.ankn.uaf.edu).

Used with permission from The Alaskan Native Knowledge Network - http://www.ankn.uaf.edu/standards/NurturingYouth.html

References
Table of References

INTRODUCTION

(1) Duran, E. & Duran, B. (1995). Native american postcolonial psychology. State University of New York Press, Albany
(2) Heylighen, F. (1997). Occam's Razor. Principia Cybernetica Web Accessed: July 9, 2002 @ http://pespmc1.vub.ac.be/OCCAMRAZ.html
(3) Stinking Thinking Anonymous, Inc. (2000). Accessed: July 9, 2002 @ http://www.stinkingthinking.com/page1.htm
(4) Burney, R. (2002). Stinking Thinking. Accessed: July 9, 2002 @ http://joy2meu.com/column.htm

RULE #1

(1) Brody, H. (1982). Maps and dreams. Pantheon, N.Y.
(2) Duran, E., & Duran, B. (1995). Native american postcolonial psychology. State University of New York Press, Albany, N.Y.
(3) Helm, J., Rogers, E. and Smith, J. (1981). *Intercultural relations and cultural change in the shield and Mackenzie Borderlands*. Handbook of North American Indians, Vol. 6, Subarctic. William C. Sturtevant, general editor. June Helm, volume editor. Washington, DC: Smithsonian Institution: 146-157
(4) Hofstede, G. (1997). Cultures and organizations: Software of the mind. Intercultural cooperation and its importance for survival
(5) Kari, J. (1986). Tatl'ahwt'aenn Nenn': The headwaters people's country; Narratives of the upper ahtna athapaskans. Transcribed by James Kari. Translated by Katie John and James Kari. Fairbanks: Alaska Native Language Center, University of Alaska Fairbanks
(6) Parker Pen Company (1993). Do's and taboos around the world. 3rd Edition. Edited by Roger E. Axtel, The Benjamin Company, New York.
(7) Ross, R. (1992). Dancing with a ghost: Exploring indian reality. Webcom Limited, Ontario, Canada
(8) VanStone, J. (1974). Athapaskan adaptations: Hunters and fishers of the subarctic forests. AHM Publishing Corp.: Arlington Heights, IL

Chapter 1: WHO AND WHY?

(1) Kizzia, T. (Mar. 4, 2002). AFN weighs claim of too many tribes. In Anchorage Daily News, Anchorage, AK. Accessed: http://www.adn.com/front/story/775506p-827532c.html
(2) Laverne, V.C. (Oct. 31, 1997). Census facts for native american month. Memorandum from the U.S. Dept. of Commerce. Accessed: http://www.census.gov/Press-Release/fs97-11.html
(3) Juneau Empire, The (1998). Special Report: Between Worlds. Accessed: (Mar. 20, 2002) http://juneaualaska.com/between/corp_index.shtml
(4) Census Bureau, U.S. (2000). American Factfinder. Accessed: (Mar. 20, 2002) http://factfinder.census.gov/servlet/QTTable?ds_name=DEC_2000_SF1_U&geo_id=01000US&qr_name=DEC_2000_SF1_U_DP1
(5) I.N.A.C.(2000). Estimates: Reports from the Canadian Department of Indian and Northern Affairs. Accesed: (March 20, 2002) http://www.ainc-inac.gc.ca/pr/est/index_e.html
(6) G.A.O. (May 5, 1997). Tax policy: a report on the Indian gaming industry. Accessed: (Mar 20, 2002) http://www.unclefed.com/GAOReports/gao97-91.html

(7) Dow, C. & Gardner-Gardin, J. (April 6, 1998). Background Paper 15 1997-98   Indigenous Affairs in Australia, New Zealand, Canada, United States of America, Norway and   Sweden. Accessed: (March 25, 2002) http://www.aph.gov.au/library/pubs/bp/1997-98/98bp15.htm#Canada

(8) Purvis, A. (December 27, 1997). Our home and native land. Time: Canada. V. 150 NO. 26. Accessed: (March 25, 2002) http://www.time.com/time/magazine/1997/int/971222/canada.our_home_and_nati5.html

CHAPTER 2: PROTOCOL

(1) Protocol Advisors, Inc. (2002). On etiquette and Protocol.   Accessed: July 9, 2002 @ http://www.protocoladvisors.com/etiquette.html

(2) Kakwirakeron & Good, D. (1996). First Nations Protocol: Working with First Nations. Accessed: July 9, 2002 @ http://www.shundahai.org/Protocol.htm#3

CHAPTER 3: WHAT IS CULTURE?

(1)   Anderson, P (1999). <u>Nonverbal communication: Forms and functions</u> Mayfield Publishing Company, Mountain View, CA.

(2) Beer, J. (Mar 18, 2002). <u>Discussing Hall's, "Beyond Culture"</u>. Accessed: http://www.culture-at-work.com/cacweek2.html

(3) Bilocerkowycz, J. (Mar 18, 2002). Purpose statement Accessed: http://www.as.udayton.edu/clusters/crossculture/purposestatement.html#

Notes: For a more complete listing of North American Native languages, please see: http://www.geocities.com/Athens/9479/na.html, or http://www.autochtones.com/en/first_peoples/languages.html.

CHAPTER 4: CONTACT

(1) Wrangell St. Elias National Park. Accessed: (April 13, 2002): http://www.nps.gov/akso/akarc/cr_wrst.htm

(2) History of the Alcan Highway. Accessed (April 13, 2002): http://www.visi.com/~alcan/History.html

(3) Alaska #1. Accessed (April 13, 2002): http://www.ibiblio.org/pub/academic/history/marshall/military/mil_hist_inst/a/alaska.asc

(4) Ross, R. (1992). <u>Dancing with a ghost: Exploring indian reality</u>. Webcom Limited, Ontario, Canada

"KASKAE"

(1)   Reckord, Holly (1983) <u>Where Raven Stood</u>, Occasional paper / Anthropology and Historic Preservation, Cooperative Park Studies Unit, University of Alaska ; no.35

(2)   Conversation with Maggie Joe and Ruth Hicks during potlatch in 1991at Chistochina, AK. in response to a discussion from a paper by Holly Reckord

CHAPTER 5: HIGH CONTEXT SOCIETY?

(1) Hall, E.T. (1990). <u>Understanding cultural differences</u>, Yarmouth, ME: Intercultural Press

(2) Gorsuch, L. & Walker, D. (Spring, 1994). Non-Verbal communication in the classroom: anglo teachers and native American students. High Plains Anthropologist, V. 14, No. 1, p. 13

CHAPTER 6: THE PERSONAL CONNECTION

(1) Reckord, H., (1983) <u>That's the way we lived: Subsistence in the wrangell-st. elias national park and preserve</u>. Anthropology and Historic Preservation, Cooperative Studies Unit, University of Alaska, Fairbanks.

(2) Joe, Maggie, (1992). Personal conversation with Ahtna matriarch.

(3) Hicks, Ruth, (1992-4). Personal conversation with an Ahtna Elder.

(4) Kari, James, (1997-9). Professor Emeritus, UAF – personal conversations

(5) Fall, Jim, (8/7/2003), Anchorage Daily News, p. A8 "Headstones: Drie to identify unmarked graves"

CHAPTER 7: HISTORY, WHOSE?

(1) Ross, R. (1992). Dancing with a ghost: Exploring indian reality. Webcom Limited, Ontario, Canada

(2) Lewin, R. (Oct. 17, 1998). Young Americans, Online Archives of New Scientist. [Subscriber based archive] Accessed: March 25, 2002 Vol. 160, Issue 2156, p. 24

(3) Deloria, V. Jr. (1995). Red earth, white lies : Native americans and the myth of scientific fact New York : Scibner

(4) Thompson, R. et al (June 2000). Recent common ancestry of human Y chromosomes: Evidence from DNA sequence data. Proc. Natl. Acad. Sci. US 20 (June 2000) 97: 7360. Accessed: (April 17, 2002). http://cogweb.ucla.edu/Abstracts/Thomson_00.html

(5) Whitehouse, D. (Dec. 6, 2000). Genetic study roots humans in Africa. BBC News online. Accessed: (April 17, 2002). http://news.bbc.co.uk/hi/english/sci/tech/newsid_1058000/1058484.stm

(6) .... Genetic evidence   Present-day DNA. Accessed: (April 17, 2002). http://www.neanderthal-modern.com/genetic3.htm

(7) .... Paleoamerican origins. Encyclopedia Smithsonian Accessed: (April 18, 2002). http://www.si.edu/resource/faq/nmnh/origin.htm

(8) National Park Service, Wranglell-St. Elias NP/P Website: Native placenames Accessed: (April 18, 2002). http://www.wrangell.st.elias.national-park.com/info.htm#ala

(9) Gee, H. (Mar. 29, 2000). Neanderthal DNA confirms distinct history. Nature Magazine. Accessed: (April 18, 2002) http://www.nature.com/nsu/000330/000330-8.html

(10) Duerinck, K. (Revised April 13, 2002). Genetics and human migration patterns. Accessed: (April 18, 2002) http://www.duerinck.com/migrate.html

(11) Torroni A, Neel JV, Barrantes R, Schurr TG, Wallace DC. (1993). Mitochondrial DNA "clock" for the Amerinds and its implications for timing their entry into North America. - Am J Hum Genet 1993 Sep: 53(3):591-608. Accessed: (April 18, 2002). http://www.chattanooga.net/cita/mtdna.html

(12) Merriwether, D. & Ferrell, R. (1995). Protein & Nucleic acid sequence analysis. American Journal of Physical Anthropology. 98, 411-30 Accessed: (April 18, 2002). http://www.psc.edu/science/Merri/merri.html

(13) ... Selected Death Tolls for Wars, Massacres and Atrocities Before the 20th Century Accessed: (April 18, 2000) http://users.erols.com/mwhite28/warstat0.htm#America

(14) Denevan, W. (1992). The native population of the Americas in 1492. University of Wisconsin Press, p. 3

FIGURE 25-1
Sources: http://www.psc.edu/science/Merri/merri.html, http://www.duerinck.com/migrate.html, http://www.faseb.org/genetics/ashg00/f1284.htm, http://www.unl.edu/rhames/courses/greenberg.htm, http://www.neanderthal-modern.com/genetic3.htm,

CHAPTER 8: CONSENSUS
(1).... Tribal justice systems. National Tribal Justice Resource Center . Tribal Justice. Accessed: (April 17, 2002). http://www.tribalresourcecenter.org/pages/justice.htm

CHAPTER 9: CULTURAL & INTELLECTUAL PROPERTY

(1) Greaves, T. (1994). <u>Intellectual property rights for indigenous peoples: A sourcebook.</u> Society for Applied Anthropology, Oklahoma City, OK

(2) Posey, D & Dutfield, G. (????). Beyond intellectual property: toward traditional resource rights for indigenous peoples and local communities. International Development Research Centre, Ottawa, Canada

(3) Brush, S. & Stabinsky, D. eds. (1996). Valuing local knowledge. Island Press, Washington, D.C. Clute, M. (Mar. 2000). Respecting native knowledge. Natural Foods Merchandiser. Accessed: (April 17, 2002). <u>http://www.healthwellexchange.com/nfm-online/nfm_backs/Mar_00/indigenous.cfm</u>

CHAPTER 10: DRESS

(1) Anderson, P (1999). <u>Nonverbal communication: Forms and functions</u> Ch. 12, Mayfield Publishing Company, Mountain View, CA.

CHAPTER 11: EDUCATION

(1) Annett, K. (1998). <u>Hidden from history: The Canadian holocaust.</u> Accessed: (Mar. 20, 2002) <u>http://members.shaw.ca/kevinannett/</u>

(2) ....Growing Apples: Abuse at church-run, native residential schools in Canada. Accessed: (April 17, 2000). <u>http://www.religioustolerance.org/sch_resid.htm</u>

(3) Philips, S. (1983).<u>The invisible culture: Communication in classroom and community on the warm springs indian reservation</u>. Waveland Press, Inc., Prospect Heights, Illinois.

CHAPTER 12: FAMILY

(1) Philips, S. (1983).<u>The invisible culture: Communication in classroom and community on the warm springs indian reservation</u>. Waveland Press, Inc., Prospect Heights, Illinois.

(2) Duran, E. & Duran, B. (1995). <u>Native american postcolonial psychology</u>. State University of New York Press, Albany

(3) Pepper, F. (1991). An indian perspective of self-esteem. Found in the Canadian Journal of Native Education, Vol. 18-2

CHAPTER 13: CLANS, MOIETIES & PHATRIES

(1) The Menominee Clan System. Accessed July 7, 2002 @ <u>http://www.menominee.com/treaty/clans.html</u>

(2) Milwaukie Public Museum (1999). Kinship-Indian County Wisconsin Accessed: July 7, 2002 @ <u>http://www.mpm.edu/wirp/ICW-48.html</u>

(3) The Ojibway Clan System, Accesed July 7, 2002 at <u>http://www.nald.ca/CLR/chikiken/page23.htm</u>

(4) Jacobs, J. (1999) <u>Post-Contact Social Organization of Three Apache Tribes</u>. Accessed: July 7, 2002 @ <u>http://www.jqjacobs.net/southwest/apache.html</u>

(5) Lippi, R. (2001). Some Basic Anthropological Terms and Concepts for ANT 314. Accessed: July 7, 2002 @ <u>http://www.marathon.uwc.edu/anthropology/gloss314.htm</u>

(6) O'Neill, D. (2002). Descent Groups Accessed: July 7, 2002 @ <u>http://anthro.palomar.edu/kinship/kinship_3.htm</u>

(7) The Columbia Encyclopedia, Sixth Edition. (2001) Columbia University Press. Accessed: July 7, 2002 @ <u>http://www.bartelby.com/65/cl/clan.html</u>

CHAPTER 14: GIFTING

(1) Brant, Dr. Clare (Jan. 9, 1982). Living, loving, hating families in the '80's. Address delivered at the Oshweken Community Hall. Oshweken, Ontario

CHAPTER 15: LANGUAGE

(1) Annett, K. (1998). Hidden from history: The Canadian holocaust. Accessed: (Mar. 20, 2002) http://members.shaw.ca/kevinannett/

(2) Philips, S. (1983).The invisible culture: Communication in classroom and community on the warm springs indian reservation. Waveland Press, Inc., Prospect Heights, Illinois.

CHAPTER 16: **NON-INTERFERENCE**

(1) Brant, Dr. Clare (Jan. 9, 1982). Living, loving, hating families in the '80's. Address delivered at the Oshweken Community Hall. Oshweken, Ontario

CHAPTER 17: **HUMOR**

(1) Jacobson, S. (1984). Central yup'ik and the schools; A handbook for teachers. .Alaska Native Language Center, U. of Alaska, Fairbanks, Fairbanks, AK

(2) National Museum of the American Indian (Mar. 11, 2002). Coyote bites back: Indian humor. Accessed: http://www.nativetelecom.org/realmedia/nmai/ndnhumor.ram

(3) Personal conversations with Linda Moreau on her time with the Little Red River Cree Nation in northern Alberta, Canada.

GGAX DADEGHAE

CHAPTER 18: **OBSERVATION**

(1) U.S Fish & Wildlife, Arctic Refuge, Where do the moose go? : Solving a moose migration mystery. Accessed: (April 11, 2002) http://www.r7.fws.gov/nwr/arctic/moosesdy.html

(2)   Bartalucci, A. & Weinstein, B. ( ) Alces, alces, U. of Michigan, Animal Diversity Web. Accessed: (April 11, 2002) http://animaldiversity.ummz.umich.edu/accounts/alces/a._alces$narrative.html

(3) http://www.taalces.net/cptmoose/facts.html

(4) Philips, S. (1983).The invisible culture: Communication in classroom and community on the warm springs indian reservation. Waveland Press, Inc., Prospect Heights, Illinois.

(5)   Swisher, K.(1994). An indian learning styles survey. Accessed (April 25, 2002) http://www.ncbe.gwu.edu/miscpubs/jeilms/vol13/americ13.htm The Journal of Educational Issues of Language Minority Students, v. 13 pp. 59-77

Chapter 19: **PATRONAGE**

(1)

CHAPTER 20: **POLITENESS**

(2) Ross, R. (1992). Dancing with a ghost: Exploring indian reality. Webcom Limited, Ontario, Canada

(3) Davies, F. (1973). Inside Intuition. p.137 McGraw-Hill

(4)   Scollon, R & Scollon, S. (1981). Interethnic Communication. Alaska Native Language Center, U. of Alaska, Fairbanks, Alaska

(5)   Jacobson, S. (1984). Central Yup'ik and the schools: discourse and non-verbal communication. Alaska Native Language Center, Fairbanks, AK.

(6) Philips, S. (1983).The invisible culture: Communication in classroom and community on the warm springs indian reservation. Waveland Press, Inc., Prospect Heights, Illinois.

(7) Attla, C. (1990). K'etetaalkkaane the one who paddled among the people and animals. Yukon Koyukuk School district/Alaska Native Language Center, Fairbanks p. xi
Baxter, E (1978) Non-verbal communication among inuit in northern canada. Found in Anthropological Papers of the University of Alaska, Vol. 19-1, June, 1978, University of Alaska Press, Fairbanks, AK.

CHAPTER 21: **NON-VERBAL**

(1) Mestel, R (April 27, 1996). <u>Behind the mask</u>. Online Archives of New Scientist. [Subscriber based archive] Accessed: March 25, 2002 Vol. 150, Issue 2027, p. 10

(2) Jacobson, S. (1984). <u>Central Yup'ik and the schools: discourse and non-verbal communication</u>. Alaska Native Language Center, Fairbanks, AK.

(3) Burgoon, J; Buller, D.; Woodall, W. (1995). <u>Non Verbal Communication: The unspoken dialogue.</u> Second Edition. McGraw-Hill Higher Education. p. 349

(4) Gorsuch, L. & Walker, D. (Spring, 1994). Non-Verbal communication in the classroom: anglo teachers and native American students. High Plains Anthropologist, V. 14, No. 1

(5) Philips, S. (1983).<u>The invisible culture: Communication in classroom and community on the warm springs indian reservation</u>. Waveland Press, Inc., Prospect Heights, Illinois.

TSIN'AEN, UGHELI KULAEN

(1) Ahtna Dictionary

CHAPTER 22: POWER & RESPECT

CHAPTER 23: SILENCE AND PATIENCE

(1) Burgoon, J; Buller, D.; Woodall, W. (1995). Non Verbal Communication: The unspoken dialogue. Second Edition. McGraw-Hill Higher Education.

(2) Gorsuch, L. & Walker, D. (Spring, 1994). Non-Verbal communication in the classroom: anglo teachers and native American students. <u>High Plains Anthropologist</u>, V. 14, No. 1

(3) Scollon, R & Scollon, S. (1981). <u>Interethnic Communication</u>. Alaska Native Language Center, U. of Alaska, Fairbanks, Alaska.

(4) Personal communication and meetings with Jack Justin of Chistochina, AK 1990-1992

CHAPTER 24: <u>SPIRITUALITY</u>

CHAPTER 25: SMELL

(1) Panati, Charles (1989). <u>Panati's extraordinary endings of practically everything and everybody</u>. P. 168 Harper & Row, N.Y.

(2) Hughs, Howard Medical Institute (Mar. 28, 2001). <u>The Mystery of smell</u>
http://www.hhmi.org/senses/d/d110.htm

(3) Hughs, Howard Medical Institute (Mar. 28, 2001). <u>A Secret sense in the human nose?</u>
http://www.hhmi.org/senses/d/d210.htm

(4) Davis, Flora (1981). <u>Inside Intuition</u> , McGraw-Hill, N.Y.

(5) Ariniello, L (1995). <u>Brain briefings; Smell and the olfactory system</u>, Society for Neuroscience. Accessed at www.sfn.org/briefings/smell.html

(6) Aoyama, S. (Mar. 3, 2001), <u>The role of the sense of smell in language learning</u>. School for International Training. p. 3 Accessed: http://leahi.kcc.hawaii.edu/org/tec_conf96/aoyama.html

(7) Wilke, M (1995). <u>Scent of a market</u>. American Demographics

(8) Aroma Systems, (Mar. 5, 2001). Examples of Environmental Fragrancing. Accessed: www.abpi.net/T2007/papers/et/docs/function.htm

(9) Naturex, (March 5, 2001). About Naturex. Accessed: http://www.naturex.ca/about.html

(10) Associated Business Publications International, <u>Military/Commercial Environmental Conditioning</u>. Accessed: http://www.abpi.net/T007/papers/docs/function.htm

(11) Anderson, P. (1999). <u>Nonverbal communication: Forms and functions</u>. Mayfield Publishing Company, Mountain View, CA.

(12) Browning, J (1999). <u>Introduction to the desana indian culture</u>. Accessed: http://www.saintmarys.edu/~berdayes/vincehome/courses/comm350/notes/olfactics.html

(13) .... (May 9. 2002). U.S. Non-lethal weapons
report suppressed. New Scientist, May 11, 2002 Issue Accessed: (May 9, 2002).
http://www.newscientist.com/news/news.jsp?id=ns99992254

CHAPTER 26: TIME

(1) Anderson, P (1999). Nonverbal communication: Forms and functions Mayfield
Publishing Company, Mountain View, CA.

(2) Knapp, M. & Hall, J. (1997). Nonverbal communication in human interaction. Harcort Brace
Publishers, Ft. Worth, TX p. 121

(3) Kairos Education, http://www.kairos.com.au/kairos.html accessed: Feb 7, 2002

(4) Massey, Lance, http://cicero.smsu.edu/journal/articles97/massey.html Accessed: Feb 7, 2002.
Journal of Public Affairs, Southwest Missouri University.

(5) Bolen, J (1979). The tao of psychology Harper & Row, San Francisco p. 93

(6) Hall, E.T. (1990). Understanding cultural differences. P. 179, Intercultural Press, Yarmouth,
ME.

(7) Scollon, R & Scollon, S. (1981). Interethnic Communication. Alaska Native Language Center,
U. of Alaska, Fairbanks, Alaska.

(8) Lewis, O. & Redish, L. Native Languages of the Americas. Accessed: (April 18, 2002).
http://www.geocities.com/bigorrin/iaq.htm#11

(17) Hampden-Turner, C & Trompenaars, F. (2000). Building cross-cultural competence: How to
create wealth from conflicting values. Yale University Press, New Haven

CHAPTER 27: ELDERS

EPILOGUE:

Notes: Some current examples

(1) Elliott, J. Oct. 30, 1995). Oh, Canada... Albion Monitor Commentary Accessed: Apr. 02, 2002
http://www.monitor.net/monitor/10-30-95/nativecanada.html

(1) Nickson, E. (2002). Every blade of grass is ours. An article about the West Coast Warriors
Society headed by David Dennis. Found in the National Post, Mar. 30, 2002, p. B2

(2) Gray, J. (2002). The chief's justice. Interview with Matthew Coon Come, National Chief of the
assemble of first nations. In Elm Street Magazine, April, 2002 p. 74-88

(3) Deer Eastern Door, K., (2002) . RCMP secret report dangerous. In the Canadian Aboriginal
website. Accessed: April 2, 2002 http://www.canadianaboriginal.com/opinion/news4e.htm \

Other Publications by the Author

The Peer Counseling Handbook: A Compendium of Themes, 1987, WCW Publishing – out of print

The Peer Counseling Manual, 1989, Options of Oregon, out of print

The Oral Tradition, 1980-2009, Newsletter, Discontinued

Healthy Alaskans 2010: Creating Healthy Communities – Contributor, 2002, State of Alaska Publication

About the Author

Gifted or cursed with inexhaustible curiosity, an admitted wanderer who rarely schedules and with an inveterate desire to learn what makes us all tick, Chris is, or has been, a lot of things

from a hippie organic farmer to prison guard, a Tribal administrator, an Alaskan, a State Planner and a Mental Health Counselor – plus many jobs from aircraft sheet metal to laborer to gold panner.

He is a graduate of Southern Oregon University (a long time ago) with a degree in Psychology and Criminology and the University of Alaska, Fairbanks with a Masters in Cross-cultural Studies. As might be expected, he tends to get the experience first and the academic parts afterwards – a bit of a contrarian.

He lives in rural, interior Alaska near the confluence of two great and powerful rivers.

www.ingramcontent.com/pod-product-compliance
Lightning Source LLC
Chambersburg PA
CBHW081353280526
45788CB00009B/2859